Spiritual Care in Public Institutions in Europe. Vol. 2

Kirche und Recht – Beihefte

Herausgegeben von
Dipl.-Kfm. Dr. iur. Jörg Antoine, Esther van Bebber, M.A., Bernd Th. Drößler, Prof. Dr. Burkhard Kämper, Dr. Jörg Kruttschnitt, Dr. Evelyne D. Menges L.I.C., Prof. Dr. Arno Schilberg, Prof. Dr. Gernot Sydow, M.A.

Beihefte, Band 11

www.steiner-verlag.de/brand/Kirche-und-Recht

Jiří Rajmund Tretera and Záboj Horák (eds.)

Spiritual Care in Public Institutions in Europe. Vol. 2

Berliner Wissenschafts-Verlag

This book was written as part of Charles University's Cooperatio research program, research field Law, research area Legal History and Roman Law.

Bibliografische Information der Deutschen Nationalbibliothek:
Die Deutsche Nationalbibliothek verzeichnet diese Publikation in der Deutschen Nationalbibliografie; detaillierte bibliografische Daten sind im Internet über dnb.d-nb.de abrufbar.

Ein Imprint der Franz Steiner Verlag GmbH
Maybachstraße 8, 70469 Stuttgart
service@steiner-verlag.de
www.steiner-verlag.de

Satz: DTP + TEXT Eva Burri, Stuttgart
Druck: docupoint, Magdeburg
Gedruckt auf säurefreiem, alterungsbeständigem Papier.
Printed in Germany.

ISBN Print 978-3-8305-5628-2
ISBN E-Book 978-3-8305-5643-5
DOI 10.35998/9783830556435

Table of contents

JIŘÍ RAJMUND TRETERA
Introductory Report 7

PIOTR STANISZ
Spiritual Care in Public Institutions in Poland
New Context and Challenges 11

FRANCIS MESSNER
Religion in French Schools
Between Spiritual Assistance and the Teaching of Religion 21

VOJTECH VLADÁR
Pastoral Care of the Catholic Church in the Armed Forces and Armed Units of the Slovak Republic 33

MARK HILL KC
Chaplaincy in England 49

FELIX HAMMER
Spiritual Care in Public Institutions in the Federal Republic of Germany and its Federal States (Länder)
Provisions in Constitutions and Treaties between State and Church and Practical Realization 59

BEATRICE SERRA
Religious Assistance in Spain
Some Notes with Special Attention to the Condition of Migrants 73

ANDREAS KOWATSCH
Spiritual Care in Public Hospitals and Care Facilities in Austria 83

HARALD TRIPP
Spiritual Care to Austrian Armed Forces-Assessment of the Current
Situation and Perspectives with Regard to Religious Law 103

STEFAN MÜCKL
Spiritual Care in Public Institutions in Italy 115

ZÁBOJ HORÁK
Changes in Spiritual Care in the Czech Republic since 2019 123

Introductory Report

JIŘÍ RAJMUND TRETERA

Ladies and Gentlemen,

As a professor of church law at the Faculty of Law of Charles University, as the President of the Church Law Society and as a priest at the head of the Pastoral Care of Lawyers in Prague, I would like to welcome you on behalf of all three of these organisations, which are the organisers of the international conference entitled Prague Dialogues on Church and State Relations. We are delighted to be able to welcome you to this year's Prague Dialogues, now in their fifth season.

In choosing the name of this regular scholarly meeting we were inspired by the name of a much larger gathering in Germany, which Associate Professor Záboj Horák and I have been attending regularly for a quarter of a century. This is the *Essener Gespräche zum Thema Staat und Kirche*, which is organised every year by the Bishopric of Essen in the Wolfsburg Catholic Academy in Mülheim an der Ruhr. However, the Prague Dialogues differ from the Essener Gespräche in that our gatherings are less frequent and the number of participants is smaller. In contrast, our sessions are longer and lectures are given by a greater number of participants. We hope that the attendees at the Prague Dialogues have more opportunity to enjoy the beautiful city of Prague, which is one of Europe's and indeed the world's major tourist destinations!

The first session of Prague Dialogues was devoted to *Church Financing in Europe and the USA*, the second to *Religion and Concordat Law of Poland, Slovakia, Hungary and the Czech Republic*, and the third to *Religion Law in Germany and the USA*.

The topic of the fourth conference in 2019 was *Spiritual Care in Public Institutions*. Representatives from the United Kingdom, France, Germany, Switzerland, Austria, Hungary, Slovakia, Poland and three representatives from the Czech Republic spoke about spiritual care in their own countries. This year, in addition, there are representatives from Italy and Spain, three speakers from Austria and four from the Czech Republic. No representatives were able to come this time from Switzerland or Hungary, and none of the invited representatives from the USA could attend.

The results of the fourth conference were published in English in the book *Spiritual Care in Public Institutions in Europe*, which was published by Berliner Wissenschafts-Verlag in 2019.

Our intention was to repeat the theme of the 2019 conference every second or third year. But alas! The Covid pandemic put a stop to that. And so, we decided to hold the 5th Prague Dialogues in 2024. Five years have at least passed since the last conference and those of us who gave talks in 2019 can focus in particular on changes in spiritual care in public institutions in our countries and their development in recent times.

This topic is of particular interest in the Czech Republic, especially since spiritual care in public institutions was restored after the fall of the communist regime in 1989. This spiritual care was rebuilt step by step.

Every year, the number of chaplains and other spiritual care workers in all sectors is growing in this country. Numerous publications are focused on the legal regulation of this care. Many articles have been published primarily by the Church Law Society in Prague in its *Church Law Review*.

For more than twenty-five years, a full-day conference on religion law has been held at the Faculty of Law of Masaryk University in Brno every September, organised by the Department of Constitutional Law and Political Science, in cooperation with the Church Law Society. The most recent conferences have dealt with individual sectors of spiritual care in public institutions.

The Czech Republic will be represented by several papers. Professor Damián Němec from the Saints Cyril and Methodius Faculty of Theology, Palacký University in Olomouc, will outline the issue of Spiritual Care in Health Care Facilities. This kind of care is still in its early days in the Czech Republic and its regulation has to overcome many difficulties. Therefore, it is appropriate to pay attention to it in a special paper.

Associate Professor Záboj Horák from Prague will talk about other sectors. And Dr Adam Csukás, our close collaborator and main lawyer of the Evangelical Church of Czech Brethren, the second largest Church in the Czech Republic, will focus on his church's participation in spiritual care in public institutions, particularly in the Evangelical Diaconia, which has expanded its activities considerably in recent years.

Other canon law and religion law teachers from Czech universities have been invited to this conference. We look forward to their participation in the discussion. We expect the same from representatives of public institutions, who have also accepted our invitation.

Eleven students of the Master and Doctoral degree programmes at the Faculty of Law of Charles University and members of the Church Law Society will be present as well, as will nine students from Vienna University in Austria.

At the present time, seven courses on canon and religion law are taught at the Faculty of Law in Prague to hundreds of students. Two scientific seminars are open, each for fifteen students, every semester. These subjects are currently taught at the Faculty of Law by four professors, who are also present at the conference.

We are looking forward to all the papers to be given by foreign and Czech participants and to the discussion to which all people present are invited.

Ladies and Gentlemen, thank you for your attention.

Editorial remark: Ten speakers have promised that their contributions will be included in the collective monograph as a development of the ideas contained in their conference contributions. And so it happened, and we can happily state that the collective monograph can go to print. *This book was written as part of Charles University's Cooperation research program, research field Law, research area Legal History and Roman Law.*

Spiritual Care in Public Institutions in Poland
New Context and Challenges

PIOTR STANISZ

I. Introduction

In a recent article dedicated to religious freedom in Poland, the author pointed out that knowledge of the Polish constitutional or statutory provisions is not enough to understand the level of religious freedom guaranteed and the actual church-state relations in Poland. The author claimed that the law reveals its real content only in its application, and this is especially true in reference to Poland in recent years. As a consequence, to understand the Polish 'law in action', it is necessary to take the broader context into account.[1]

Despite the possible objections to this claim (the first of which is that under the regime of the democratic state ruled by law, it should be the law, among other things, that is supposed to shape people's behaviours and not otherwise), a careful observer of public life must recognise that significant changes have taken place in Poland recently. This new context has impacted not only church-state relations in general but also religious freedom in its different aspects. The issue of pastoral care in public institutions is no exception here. Although the relevant provisions have not changed in the past few years, it is difficult to conclude without hesitation that public authorities in Poland currently 'demonstrate considerable sensitivity to the right of every person to religious assistance and the connected right of religious communities to ensure this assistance to their members'.[2] Thus, the aim of the present paper is to discuss the reasons for this state of affairs and the resulting challenges.

---

1 See *Brzozowski,* La libertà religiosa in Polonia nello specchio della giurisprudenza, in Quaderni di diritto e politica ecclesiastica 2024, n. 1, p. 187–188.

2 *Stanisz,* Spiritual Care in Public Institutions in Poland: Searching for a Balanced Model, in *Tretera/ Horák* (eds.), Spiritual Care in Public Institutions in Europe, 2019, Berlin, p. 96.

II. Current situation

In the period of the so-called People's Poland (1945–1989), the issue of pastoral activity in hospitals, prisons and the Armed Forces permanently constituted a bone of contention between the state and the Catholic Church. A large majority of society professed Catholicism, but the state policy pursued at that time, which was based on Soviet models, rested on anti-religious assumptions; the church was recognised as a 'class enemy' and became subject to repression. As a result, generally, there was no place for religious elements in public institutions. However, owing to the constant pressure from the Polish Episcopate, chaplains were gradually but reluctantly allowed to minister to the sick in hospitals or to prison inmates. Military pastoral care was a separate issue. The fragile structures of military chaplaincies that formally existed throughout the period of People's Poland were subordinated to the state authorities to an extent that undermined their dependence on the bishops. In this situation, it was obvious that after the downfall of the communist regime, the establishment of permanent pastoral structures in hospitals, penitentiaries and the military was given priority.[3]

The Act of 17 May 1989 on the Guarantees of Freedom of Conscience and Belief ensured the right of every person (including soldiers, inmates and hospital patients) to participate in religious practices, carry out religious duties and celebrate religious holidays in accordance with the principles of their religion (Article 2.2). To secure the effectiveness of this right, religious organisations were guaranteed the right to provide religious services (also to persons belonging to the three above-mentioned groups), perform rituals and hold religious gatherings (Article 19.2.3). On the basis of the ideas behind these norms, elaborate pastoral structures in various public institutions developed in the following years.[4]

In the Polish army, at present, permanent structures of the chaplaincies of the Catholic Church, Orthodox Church and the Evangelical Church of the Augsburg Confession are in place. They all have a solid foundation in the current law and are fully financed by public funds. The existence of the Catholic Military Ordinariate is guaranteed in the concordat between the Holy See and the Republic of Poland, signed on 28 July 1993 (Article 16). In reference to the Orthodox and Evangelical military chaplaincies, similar guarantees are included in the Acts on the relations be-

---

3 *Misztal/Stanisz* (eds.), Prawo wyznaniowe, 2003, Lublin, p. 318–320, 325–327, 334–339.

4 For a characterisation of the provisions pertaining to the chaplaincies in public institutions in Poland and the resulting practice, see *Stanisz* (note 2), p. 85–97; *Stanisz*, Religious Assistance in Public Institutions in Poland, in *Balodis/Blanco* (eds.), Religious Assistance in Public Institutions: Proceedings of the XXVIIIth Annual Conference (Jurmala, 13–16 October 2016), 2018, Granada, p. 275–286. The 1993 Concordat provisions pertaining to chaplaincies in public institutions are discussed by *Krukowski*, Pastoral Care of Specific Social Groups, in *Krukowski* (ed.), Concordats between the Holy See and Poland: History and the Present, 2020, Lublin, p. 291–301.

tween the state and the churches.[5] The Evangelical military chaplaincy fulfils its functions towards persons belonging not only to the Lutheran Church but also to some other protestant churches.[6] However, as stated earlier, the right to provide spiritual care to soldiers is guaranteed to all religious organisations in the Act of 17 May 1989 on the Guarantees of Freedom of Conscience and Belief (see Article 19.2.3).

Chaplains are also widely present in Polish hospitals and prisons. Their right to perform religious services to patients and inmates is ensured in a similar way as that to soldiers. However, in healthcare institutions, the formal employment of chaplains is expressly provided only in relation to the Catholic and Orthodox clergy, and in practice, most hospital chaplains are Catholic priests. The provisions pertaining to prison chaplaincy are more general in their expression, and among the chaplains employed by penitentiary institutions are Catholic, Orthodox, Evangelical and Pentecostal clergymen.

Moreover, a characteristic feature of the Polish model of state-church relations is the presence of chaplains in some other public institutions. For the most part, this is the result of special agreements between the authorities of these institutions and church representatives. Formally established Catholic, Orthodox and Evangelical chaplaincies now exist in the Border Guard; Catholic and Orthodox chaplaincies, in the National Revenue Administration; and Catholic chaplaincy, in the Police and State Fire Service. The numbers of chaplains in these structures are low. However, these chaplains have often been considered an expression of the implementation of the constitutional principle of cooperation between the state and churches. In view of this perception of chaplaincies, however, they are especially vulnerable to the effects of changes in state-church relations.

III. Constitutional model of church-state relations and the question of political will

After the experiences of subordination of the Polish law on religion to the Soviet model of state-church separation, the democratic legislator opted for the cooperation model of state-church relations, in which 'the basic separation of State and religion' is complemented by the recognition of 'a multitude of common tasks in the fulfilment of which State and religious activity are linked'.[7] In consequence, in Ar-

---

5 See Articles 21–24 of the Act of 4 July 1991 on the Relations between the State and the Polish Autocephalous Orthodox Church; Articles 29–31 of the Act of 13 May 1994 on the Relations between the State and the Evangelical Church of the Augsburg Confession in the Republic of Poland.

6 It pertains to the Evangelical Reformed Church, Evangelical Methodist Church, Church of Christian Baptists and the Seventh-day Adventist Church.

7 *Robbers*, State and Church in the European Union, in *Robbers* (ed.), State and Church in the European Union, 2019, Baden-Baden, p. 679.

ticle 25 of the Polish Constitution, which complements the articulated guarantees of the freedom of conscience and religion of Article 53, we find in the first place the norms linked to the idea of state-church separation. The following principles fall into this category: equal rights of churches and other religious organisations, impartiality of public authorities in matters of personal convictions and autonomy and independence in state-church relations. In addition, the Constitution enumerates the principle of cooperation of the state and religious organisations for the good of the human person and the common good, and the principle of consensual regulation of their mutual relations (concordat for the Catholic Church and national public law agreements pertaining to the relations between the state and non-Catholic religious organisations).[8]

The important difference between the norms in the two groups is the significance of political will in their application. In any of the enumerated norms, there is some 'margin of appreciation'. Nevertheless, the role of political will is especially important in reference to the principles of collaboration and bilateralism. It is impossible to imagine engaged collaboration without political will; without political will, any agreement could be concluded. The current situation in Poland could be defined as a withdrawal of public authorities to the separationist positions because political will, which is necessary for the realisation of collaboration and mutual agreements with religious organisations, appears to be lacking. This indicates an unfavourable change in the rules for the teaching of religion in schools, which have governed the organisation of religious instruction within the Polish educational system for more than 30 years. The change is the result of the regulation of 26 July 2024 of the Minister of Education, which, in violation of Article 12(2) of the Act of 7 September 1991 on the School Education System, was issued without an agreement with the authorities of churches and other religious organisations.[9]

IV. Government coalition towards the Catholic Church

The current political situation is a result of the parliamentary election of 2023. The Law and Justice Party (*Prawo i Sprawiedliwość*), which was in government for the last 8 years, despite gaining 35.5 % of the votes in the *Sejm* election,[10] was incapable of creating a government coalition and passed to the opposition. The government

---

8 For the characterisation of the Polish constitutional model of state-church relations, see *Stanisz*, Religion and Law in Poland, 2023, Alphen aan den Rijn, p. 35–43.

9 See *Stanisz/Walencik*, Tryb nowelizacji rozporządzenia Ministra Edukacji Narodowej z dnia 14 kwietnia 1992 r. w sprawie warunków i sposobu organizowania nauki religii w publicznych przedszkolach i szkołach, in Studia z Prawa Wyznaniowego 2024, vol. 27 (in print).

10 For the 2023 election results, see https://sejmsenat2023.pkw.gov.pl/sejmsenat2023/pl (accessed 14 Sep 2024).

majority has been formed by three other political groups (the Civic Coalition with the primary position of the Civic Platform, the Third Way and the New Left) whose primary bond was a desire to remove the Law and Justice Party from power. Consequently, their election programs were in clear opposition to the agenda implemented over the past 8 years until 2023. This also applies to ethical and moral issues (abortion, *in vitro* procedures, recognition of partnerships, etc.) and state-church relations. On all these issues, the Law and Justice Party presented a traditionalist position very close to the position of the Catholic Church. This in itself created the impression of a kind of throne-altar alliance, which was reinforced by official declarations by some Catholic hierarchs and the widespread knowledge of the generous support given to some Catholic initiatives by the public authorities of that time.

The Constitutional Court's judgement of 22 October 2020 (K 1/20), which put an end to the so-called abortion compromise, also significantly contributed to the radicalisation of sentiments.[11] This judgement caused numerous protests inspired by the All-Poland Women's Strike. They were often targeted not only against the government of that time but also sometimes against the Church, perceived as a kind of driving force.[12]

The last important factor that should be taken into account concerns loud cases of paedophilia among the clergy. This painful phenomenon has also its important financial aspect because the Supreme Court in two recent judgements imposed heavy financial responsibility on church institutions.[13]

All the factors undermined social trust in the Catholic Church and its social position. Simultaneously, government policy, which focused on settling accounts with the previous government and revising previous priorities, turned against the (authentic and alleged) privileges of the church.

V. Financing of the church in election programmes

The current majority of government parties have built their success, among other things, on different slogans pertaining to the position of the church. Only the Polish Peasant Party, which belongs to the Third Way, has been an exception in this regard. The postulates pertaining to church financing were present in the election

---

11 The Constitutional Court ruled that abortion for embryo-pathological reasons is not compatible with the Polish Constitution. For a critical commentary, see *Młynarska-Sobaczewska*, Unconstitutionality of Access to Abortion for Embryo-Pathological Reasons, in International Human Rights Law Review 2021, vol. 10, issue 1, p. 168–179.

12 See Stanisz (note 8), p. 101–102.

13 See the Supreme Court judgements of 31 March 2020 (II CSK 124/19; *Lex*) and 6 September 2022 (II CSKP 466/22; *Lex*).

programmes of all other parties that now create the government. All these postulates emphasised the need to diminish the state's engagement in the financing of church institutions and clergy. One programme (2050 Poland) even included the abolishment of some official chaplaincies, stating that 'chaplains will only be allowed in the Armed Forces, Police and Border Guard'.[14]

Recently, two new political initiatives have been launched. In March, the speaker of the Sejm requested the audit of public financing of religious organisations by the Supreme Audit Office.[15] In May, the leader of the New Left filed a parliamentary question to the prime minister about the scope and amount of public funding to religious organisations.[16] Both expressly referred to the chaplaincies in public institutions. It seems clear that in the near future, the government will propose a draft of important changes to the rules of financing religious organisations in Poland.

VI. Social changes

The current political scene is a reflection of social changes. Polish society is becoming much less uniform from a religious perspective than a few decades before. In the last 30 years, the percentage of believers has decreased from 94 % (in 1992) to 78 % (in 2024), and non-believers has increased to 14 % of the population. The percentage of regular practitioners (those who attend religious services at least once a week) has decreased to 34 % (and to nearly 24 % in big cities). Especially significant is the so-called age gap in religious commitment in Poland. Only one of five young Poles attend religious services at least once a week, and the percentage of total non-practitioners is higher than 40 points in this group.[17] On the basis of

---

14 See polska2050.pl/polska-2050-program-trzecia-droga-to-programy-a-nie-klotnie/rozdzial-kosciola-od-panstwa-koniec-pedofilii-i-funduszu-koscilenego/ (accessed 14 Sep 2024).

15 See Marszałek Sejmu zlecił NIK kontrolę finansowania kościołów i związków wyznaniowych ze środków publicznych, www.sejm.gov.pl/Sejm10.nsf/komunikat.xsp?documentId=751DA21995BEED5EC1258AE10032A1AB (accessed 14 Sep 2024).

16 See Interpelacja nr 2851 w sprawie zakresu i wysokości wsparcia ze środków publicznych dla kościołów i innych związków wyznaniowych, sejm.gov.pl/Sejm10.nsf/interpelacja.xsp?typ=INT&nr=2851 (accessed 14 Sep 2024).

17 See *Centrum Badania Opinii Społecznej*, Religijność Polaków w ostatnich dziesięcioleciach. Komunikat z badań (nr 50/2024), 2024, Warszawa, www.google.com/url?sa=t&source=web&rct=j&opi=89978449&url=https://www.cbos.pl/SPISKOM.POL/2024/K_050_24.PDF&ved=2ahUKEwiEl7XT3cSIAxVIA9sEHQqNFLcQFnoECBQQAw&usg=AOvVaw19fUqTGiZjBrC9jnB8gpZ (accessed 14 Sep 2024); *Centrum Badania Opinii Społecznej*, Polski pejzaż religijny – z dalekiego planu. Komunikat z badań (nr 89/2022), 2022, Warszawa, www.google.com/url?sa=t&source=web&rct=j&opi=89978449&url=https://www.cbos.pl/SPISKOM.POL/2022/K_089_22.PDF&ved=2ahUKEwishrOK3sSIAxVSSvEDHSKJI7sQFnoECAgQAQ&usg=AOvVawoQjyevGRfjQWmn14GFVPpF (accessed 14 Sep 2024).

a study by the Pew Research Center in 2018, Poland is a worldwide leader in terms of the difference in religiousness between the younger and older generations. In worship attendance, the difference between adults younger and those older than 40 years is 29 %; and in daily prayer, the difference is 25 %.[18]

VII. Challenges

In the described situation, the Catholic Church in Poland faces the crucial challenge of regaining authority and social trust. Especially important from the government's perspective is to objectify both the allegation against the church and the demands for change in the legal position of the church. The distinction between due rights, expressions of good will and undue privileges is of fundamental importance in this process. The rights should be guaranteed by the state and defended by believers and religious communities. The undue privileges should be eliminated by the state and renounced with no regrets by religious communities. In turn, the space for expressions of goodwill should be managed carefully.

Defining the rights that should be protected and defended is the most important task in this regard. The Polish Constitution clearly states that the freedom of religion includes the right of individuals, wherever they are, to benefit from religious services (see Article 53.2). The basic religious rights of persons in military service, hospitalised and residing in penitentiary institutions have been acknowledged, as stated earlier, also on the statutory level and–in reference to Catholics–in the concordat. The Act of 6 November 2008 on the Rights of the Patient and Patient's Rights Advocate even states that the duty to cover expenses after from the realisation of the patient's right to religious assistance rests with the health institution (see Article 38).

From a broader perspective, the protection of 'the right to the free practice of religion in hospitals, prisons and the armed forces' should be considered a requirement of any state that protects human rights.[19] The state has even financial duties connected with the 'support for spiritual assistance which accommodates pastoral care and religious practices'.[20] These conclusions, drawn from the comparative analyses of the legislation and practices of the European Union States, are confirmed in the so-called positive obligations of the state. If the intervention of the state is necessary to secure respect for the right to freedom of thought, conscience

---

18 See *Pew Research Center,* The Age Gap in Religion around the World, www.pewresearch.org/religion/2018/06/13/the-age-gap-in-religion-around-the-world/ (accessed 14 Sep 2024).

19 It is considered one of the principles of religion law common to the states of Europe. See *Doe,* Law and Religion in Europe: A Comparative Introduction, 2011, Oxford, p. 264.

20 *Doe* (note 19), p. 264.

and religion, that is, if the individual is not able to enjoy this right without the state's support, the generally negative duties of the state to protect human rights must be complemented by its positive action.

An interesting observation is that the only case lost by Poland under Article 9 of the European Convention of Human Rights was examined by the European Court of Human Rights from the standpoint of the state's positive obligations (see the judgment of 7 December 2010 in *Jakóbski v. Poland*). The case pertained to religious practices in prison. The application regarded the refusal by prison authorities to provide the applicant with meat-free meals according to Buddhist Mahayana dietary rules. The Court concluded that there had been a breach of Article 9 because the applicant repeatedly requested a meat-free diet and the authorities refused his requests on different grounds, particularly on the grounds that preparation of such meals for one person would be too expensive. It was clear that a decision to make special arrangements for one prisoner could have some financial implications, but the question was whether the state had struck a fair balance between the interests of the institution, other prisoners and the particular interests of the applicant. The Court's answer was negative: the rights of the inmate were completely disregarded, and the interests of the penitentiary institution were overemphasised.

Obviously, it is difficult to draw precise conclusions pertaining to the organisation of chaplaincies from the cited Strasbourg judgement. However, it is justified to claim that the creation of the conditions of the free enjoyment of religious freedom by a larger group of people can result in greater expenses. The question is where to find a fair balance between competing interests, one of which is clearly the right of hospitalised or detained people, or soldiers serving in the army to enjoy religious services. The expenses that must be borne on this occasion should not be viewed as simple financing of religious communities from public funds but rather as a cost of the realisation of rights that the state is obliged to secure.

On the other hand, chaplaincy in some other public institutions can be viewed differently. Its existence can be perceived only as an expression of goodwill by the state and a sign of its collaboration with religious organisations. Some authors have even perceived it as an undue privilege and a realisation of a particular rather than a common good, which infringes some constitutional principles (the principle of mutual independence of the state and religious organisations in the first place).[21] Individuals serving in these formations (particularly in the National Revenue Administration) are apparently generally free to fulfil their religious needs and benefit from religious services, and any special arrangements by the state is not necessary in this regard.

---

21 See *Mezglewski*, Dobro wspólne czy partykularne? Uwagi na temat celów duszpasterstwa w Policji, in *Uruszczak/Krzysztofek/Mikuła (eds.)*, Kościoły i inne związki wyznaniowe w służbie dobru wspólnemu, 2014, Kraków, p. 209–219.

VIII. Conclusion

As shown by sociological data and official declarations of political party leaders, the Polish religious landscape is rapidly changing. Moreover, church-state relations are in a difficult moment, and how they will evolve in the near future is uncertain. This state of affairs can impact chaplaincies in public institutions, especially considering that this topic is clearly discussed in public debates. In this context, it is especially important to emphasise that this issue should not be perceived only as an element (and some kind of outcome) of changing institutional relations between the state and the church. It primarily pertains to human rights, especially the right to freedom of thought, conscience and religion.

Religion in French Schools
Between Spiritual Assistance and the Teaching of Religion

FRANCIS MESSNER

I. Introduction

Contrary to popular belief, the constitutional principle of secularism does not have the effect of prohibiting all religious activity in public educational establishments. On the contrary, the legal texts organizing the French educational system guarantee freedom of religious education[1].

In French law, the transmission of beliefs is one of the components of the freedom to exercise one's religion. The first article of the codified law of 31 December 1959 specifies that "the State takes all useful measures to ensure freedom of worship and religious instruction for students in public education." It establishes the guarantee of freedom of religious instruction. The State is required to promote its effective implementation through an appropriate system.

Freedom of religious instruction is implemented in French law in different ways depending on the territory, provided in all cases that this freedom can be fully exercised. In the departments covered by the law of 9 December 1905, but also in the department of Guyana and in the overseas territories where the law of 1905 does not apply, it takes the form of a day of weekly vacation for the purpose of providing catechetical teaching to children in primary schools and the creation of chaplaincies within middle and high schools or outside these establishments. In the departments of Rhine and Moselle, on the other hand, religious education is an integral part of public education curricula. Its organization is determined by local Alsatian Moselle law.

Furthermore, on another note, the teaching of religion as a subject of knowledge and a means of understanding societies[2] does not constitute a separate teaching in France but is provided within the framework of existing disciplines and more particularly history. Teachers should, as part of their initial training and continuing education, benefit from specific training under the aegis of the European Institute

---

1 *Messner (dir.)/Prélot/Woehrling,* Traité de droit français des religions, 2013, Paris, p. 1749–1818; *Fornerod,* Assistance spirituelle dans les services publics, 2012, Strasbourg.

2 *Messner,* La culture religieuse à l'école, 1995, Paris.

of Religious Sciences/IESR in Paris. The IESR linked to the Ecole Pratique des Hautes Etudes/EPHE has branches in a few academies[3]. But this awareness of teachers about religion or religious culture is based on volunteering and the courses are implemented in a very differentiated manner depending on the academies. All students, whether subject to general law or local law, are also required to follow moral and civic education.

II. Religious instruction in general law

According to statistics provided by the Catholic Church, 80 % of children in public primary schools were catechized in 1950. They were only 30 % in 2007.[4] In 2016 the newspaper La Croix reported that 17 % of children were catechized in primary schools. The share of students in public education Catholic chaplaincy (middle and high schools), which numbered 73,000 for 5,803 secondary schools in 2016, is very low.[5] There were 118,000 in 2000. Less than 4 % of middle school students and 1 % of high school students participated in chaplaincy activities in 2004. In a response to a parliamentary question in 2003, the minister put forward the following figures relating to 16 Academies (France has 30):1 685 chaplaincies including 1664 Catholics, 16 Protestants and 5 Israelites.[6]

In September 2023, the Paris rectorate/académie de Paris recognizes 150 Catholic chaplaincies attached to middle and high schools. 72 Parisian establishments do not have a Catholic chaplaincy recognized by the rectorate. The chaplaincies of public high schools and colleges were almost all created at the request of Catholic parents. Protestant families favor Sunday school taught in the annexes of the premises of their worship while the children of practicing Jewish families are, for the most part, educated in private schools where religious education is an integral part of the curriculum. There is no Muslim chaplaincy in middle and high schools in mainland France.[7] This absence is linked to the distrust of the administration and the breakdown of the Muslim community.

Currently, five chaplaincies are responsible for a chapel assigned to worship located within a public school in Paris: Henri IV, Louis-le-Grand, Saint-Louis, Mon-

---

3 *Estivalèzes,* Les religions dans l'enseignement laïque, 2005, Paris; *Borne (dir.)/Willaime,* Enseigner les faits religieux, 2007, Paris.

4 Site de la Conférence épiscopale de France. See eglise.catholique.fr/conference-des-eveques-de-france/

5 La Croix, 29 September 2016.

6 Response published in the Official Journal: 10 November 2003.

7 See www.streetpress.com/sujet/1485970096-des-centaines-d-aumoneries-l-ecole-laique-mais-zero-musulmane (accessed 25 July 2025).

taigne and Janson-de-Sailly. Other public establishments have a chapel, but which is no longer used for worship.

In private schools under contract and outside of contract, religious education is part of the programs. But students can be exempted. Catholic establishments generally offer one optional hour of denominational religious education and one compulsory hour of religious culture.

II.1 The principle of the weekly vacation in primary schools in general law

Primary education, statutorily denominational since the law of 15 March 1850 (Falloux law), was completely secularized by the law of 28 March 1882 (Ferry law), supplemented by the law of 16 June 1886 (Goblet law). Since the promulgation of these legislative texts, school has been public, free, compulsory and secular. Under the terms of articles 1 and 2 of the codified law of 28 March 1882/Code de l'éducation,[8] the content of education, the teaching staff as well as the premises of public primary schools are required to be neutral. As a result, since the end of the 19th century, religious education can no longer be provided in the premises of public primary schools.

The break with the law of March 1850 is radical. But it is appropriate to respect parents freedom of exercise of religion and "this delicate and sacred thing that is the conscience of children."[9] Thus the Education Code requires public primary schools to operate "one day per week in addition to Sunday, in order to allow parents to give their children religious education if they wish."[10]

The day left vacant for religious education will initially be set for Thursday, then transferred to Wednesday to finally be called into question with the prospect of moving it to Saturday as part of a continuous school week. Wednesday will ultimately remain and this, in accordance with the decree of 12 May 1972,[11] reserved for religious education. But the academy inspector can make adjustments to the rules thus established after consultation with the authorities responsible for activities of a cultural nature and those competent for religious teaching. An implementing circular of 24 April 1991 specifies that the adjustments must not infringe the conditions for exercising freedom of religious instruction. Note that this provision is poorly known by the various stakeholders in the school and in particular by those primarily concerned, that is to say the parents.

---

8 Article L. 141-4, Code de l'éducation.

9 *Ferry*, Lettre aux instituteurs du 17 novembre 1883.

10 Article L. 141-3, Code de l'éducation.

11 Arrêté du 12 mai 1972, published in the Official Journal : 17 mai 1972, p. 4992.

II.2 The regime of high school and college chaplaincies

The legal foundations of chaplaincy in public secondary education establishments (middle and high schools) under the separation regime are enshrined in the law of 9 December 1905. Under the terms of the first article of this text, "the Republic guarantees the freedom of conscience and worship", no one can be deprived of the right to exercise their religion because of their confinement in a public enclosure. This principle applies to chaplaincies of high school and college boarding schools (article 2, § 2, law of 9 December 1905). The administrative judge considers that religious education is one of the components of freedom of worship. Consequently, the creation of a chaplaincy is obligatory since students do not have the opportunity to exercise their religion and follow religious education outside the establishment.[12]

Alongside this status of boarding school chaplaincies, the codified law of 31 December 1959 (Debré law) provided for the possibility of establishing chaplaincies in middle and high schools,[13] even in the absence of boarding schools. The religious instruction provided in these establishments through chaplaincies concerns exclusively the freedom of conscience and worship of parents and students. It does not constitute a guaranteed right for religious denominations to organize this teaching. The legal status of chaplaincies arises from the Education Code.[14] It is explained by circulars.[15] The creation of a chaplaincy is linked for secondary establishments "to the existence of a demand from families". This religious service cannot be offered by the administration of the establishment, nor by an authority representing a religion. This is an exclusive right of parents of minor children or their legal guardians and adult students. Received by nominative requests from parents or adult students, the head of the establishment is required to transmit the request to the rector of the academy, indicating the expected numbers. In practice, the request is generally made by at least three parents. Based on the files, the rector of the academy decides each year on the creation of chaplaincy services in establishments that do not have boarding schools. The decision-making power of the rector is not linked. However, any refusal must be justified. A circular of 22 April 1988 specifies that the general rule must be to satisfy the wishes of the applicants, even if they represent only a very small percentage of the total workforce of the establishment. Furthermore, the rector has discretion over the advisability of or-

---

12 Conseil d'Etat, 28 janvier 1955, Association professionnelle des aumôniers de l'enseignement public, RecCE, p. 51.

13 *Swerry*, Aumôneries catholiques dans l'enseignement public, 1995, Paris; *Messner/Woehrling*, Les statuts de l'enseignement religieux, 1996, Paris.

14 Articles L. 141-2, R 141-2–141-7, Code de l'éducation.

15 Circulaire du Ministre de l'Education nationale, n° 88–112, 22 avril 1988.

ganizing "recognized" chaplaincy activities within the establishment rather than outside the establishment.

Religious instruction is provided by a chaplain or chaplaincy manager, that is to say a person designated by the competent religious authority to exercise this function.[16] The head of the chaplaincy and any deputies are approved by the rector. The dismissal of the chaplain occurs at the request of the rector or the religious authority. Paragraph 2 of article 2 of the law of 9 December 1905 does not prohibit the remuneration of chaplains. In practice, if it is effective for chaplains, prisons and hospitals, it is excluded for chaplains of middle and high schools, including those of boarding schools which are paid by their religions. The wearing of religious clothing by students is governed by provisions separate from those concerning chaplains. The 2004 law does not apply to chaplains.[17].

The school administration is required to inform students, or their parents when they are minors, of the existence of a chaplaincy service. The registration initiative falls to the parents for young people under 15 years old and to the latter when they are over 15 years old. This first registration does not have to be repeated from year to year. It is valid until it has been modified in writing. All of the provisions developed below also concern the BTS and CPGE/Preparatory Classes for Grandes Écoles.

The role of the Catholic chaplaincy in public schools is, according to the authorities of this religion, to transmit and educate in the Christian faith but also to provide information to students on religious questions. Finally, these chaplaincies carry out a set of cultural actions (outings, concerts, meetings, debates, etc.).

III. Religious education in schools, colleges and high schools in the Rhine and Moselle departments

The general law of chaplaincies, underpinned by the laws of "secularization" of education at the end of the 19th century, is limited to identifying mechanisms aimed at guaranteeing the freedom of conscience and worship of parents and students. This is different from local Alsatian Moselle education law, where religious education is an integral part of school programs.

The standards relating to religious education in local Alsatian-Moselle law are composite. They include texts of French origin (law of 15 March 1850 known as the Falloux law) and texts of German origin (law of 12 February 1873 on public and private education modified by an ordinance of 16 November 1887). This legal

16 Circulaire n° 79–452, 19 décembre 1979, BOEN 1979, p. 47.

17 Question n° 48655 parue au *Journal officiel*, AN, 19 octobre 2004, p. 8071 et réponse publiée au *Journal officiel*, AN, 8 février 2005, p. 1375.

arsenal, which was maintained following the return of Alsace Moselle to France, as well as subsequent texts (decree of 3 September 1974 as amended) remains in force in the departments of Rhine and Moselle in accordance with article L 481-1 of the Code of education.[18]

The amended order of 10 July 1873 provides in article 10A that "in all schools, teaching and education must tend to develop religion [...]". This text applies to both primary schools and secondary education in which he made the teaching of religion compulsory. However, this obligation is imposed differently depending on whether it is first or second degree.

III.1 Education and religion in primary schools

Under the terms of article 36 of the law of 15 March 1850 (Falloux law), public primary schools are denominational. This norm, which established separations based on religious affiliations between schools, was attenuated by article 15 which authorizes municipalities "due to circumstances and provisionally, to establish or maintain primary schools in which children of the same type will be admitted. One or the other sex, or children belonging to a different religion." There is currently no difference between denominational and interdenominational primary schools. The religious affiliation of students and teachers is no longer taken into account in the organization and operation of these establishments, with the exception of religious education. But even in this case the parents indicate the chosen course, without the administration being able to verify their religious affiliation.[19]

Confessional religious education from the Catholic and Protestant Churches as well as the Jewish faith is in fact an integral part of school programs. The student participation rate fell from 71 % in 2007 to 58 % in 2014. It is still 47 % in 2024. The Nancy Academy reports a similar participation rate for the Moselle department. This teaching set up with the agreement of the religious authorities of only statutory religions, that is to say recognized religions to the exclusion of non-statutory or unrecognized religions, is of one hour, integrated into the use of the weekly time. It is compulsory as it is linked to compulsory education in general, but parents of students can refuse registration for this education. In practice the exemption procedure has been simplified. Parents complete a registration form providing for participation in one of the religious education courses or, failing that, in a moral education course taught in the latter case by school teachers.[20] In addition to re-

---

18 The texts forming local education law remained in force initially provisionally by a law of 12 October 1919 then definitively in the absence of explicit repeal of this law by that of 1 June 1924.

19 Décret du 3 septembre 1974; décret du 6 septembre 1990.

20 Articles D. 481-2 à D 481-6, Code de l'éducation.

ligious education and alternative moral education given to students exempt from religious education, there is moral and civic education which is compulsory taught throughout France. A student exempt from religious education is required to follow a morality course and a moral and civic education course.[21]

Religious education in primary schools is, under the terms of the texts in force, denominational: Catholic, Protestant or Jewish. Interfaith religious education (Catholic and Protestant) established in certain schools is a modality of denominational religious education. Its establishment is authorized by the religious authorities of the two religions concerned who inform the school council and send a request for organization to the management of the departmental national education services. This interfaith education is not compulsory.

Religious education initially given by teachers, now school teachers, has for several decades been provided by a minister of religion or in most cases by a qualified person/Religious speaker/IDR proposed by the religious authority and paid by hourly compensation. The training of IDRs is provided by religious authorities. They are in principle required to follow the teachings created for this purpose by the faculties of Catholic and Protestant theology of the University of Strasbourg, respectively DU-FAPER and DU of the Center for Theological and Practical Training as well as the department of Catholic theology of the University of Lorraine in Metz.

Denominational religious education is an integral part of school curricula.[22] It is given by or under the supervision of the various ministers of the four statutory religions[23] and is one hour integrated into the weekly timetable. A second hour can be requested by parents, which is rather rare.

The pre-primary cycle does not include compulsory religious education. A religious awakening can, however, be organized in nursery schools by school teachers. In the absence of a volunteer teacher, religious awakening is not guaranteed, which is the case in most nursery schools.[24]

III.2 Religious education in middle and high schools

The number of students enrolled in religious education has been in constant decline in recent years. For secondary education as a whole, 21 % of students took these courses in 2013/2014, i. e. 26.31 % in middle school and 13.56 % in high school.

---

21 Question n° 36576, JOAN, 7 janvier 2014, p. 241; Bulletin officiel de l'éducation nationale, n° 30 du 26-7-2018.

22 Article 23, loi du 15 mars 1850.

23 Décret n° 74–763 du 3 septembre 1974, modifié par le décret n° 91–517 du 3 juin 1991.

24 Décret 21 mars 1855.

In 2018 the participation rate was 13.11 % for all secondary education, i. e. 16.36 % in middle schools and 8.23 % in high schools. It fell to 10 % in 2024. Religious education was not provided in 2013/14 in one middle school out of 147 and in 4 high schools out of 69. 132 FTE (full-time equivalent) position support were made available from the Strasbourg Academy in 2013/2014. They are occupied by 180 staff divided between certified staff (87 + 17 interns), contract workers (28), auxiliary teachers (9), ministers of religion (30 including 26 pastors) and a temporary worker. The large number of incumbents and future incumbents is explained by the establishment of mechanisms to reduce job insecurity in the public service. Reserved CAPES competitions were regularly organized for the benefit of auxiliary teachers and contract workers meeting certain conditions.

Secondary and technical education establishments are non-denominational but the teaching of religion for students of the four statutory religions (Catholic, Protestant, Jewish) is an integral part of the programs of these establishments. The administration is required to organize religious education.[25] Parents or adult students complete a form entitled Registration for religious education. They choose to enroll in Catholic, Protestant[26] or Jewish religious education without being required to provide proof of affiliation with the confession concerned. They can also choose not to follow religious education without having to justify their decision. Unlike primary schools, there are no substitute moral education courses in the event of non-enrollment in religious education. Registration is valid for the school year, but exemptions may be granted during the year. Religious education, 1 hour per week for an optimal group of 15 students, is normally provided in classes or groups of students of the same level. If the number of students is too low, students can be grouped together by joint level (4th/3rd; 6th/5th for example) or exceptionally over the entire course. Religious education courses are denominational. In high schools, cultural and religious awakening (CRE) constitutes a particular modality of this confessional education and as such cannot be imposed on students.

Religious education courses provided in secondary education establishments are denominational in that the programs are written under the control of religious authorities and the teachers of this subject are proposed to the administration by these same authorities for appointment. But the content of these courses is not a catechetical approach. Thus, Protestant religion teachers give religious culture courses based on the common core of knowledge and skills "while taking into account the human being in its spiritual dimension by addressing existential questions." The Protestant religious education programs structured around four

---

25 Conseil d'Etat, 6 avril 2001.

26 Recognized Lutheran and Reformed denominations commonly organize religious education in public schools.

themes: reading and approach to biblical texts, religion in the city, different religions and ethics, are validated by the UEPAL/United Protestant Church authorities. Catholic religious education programs favor a presentation of Christianity and other religions "in a reflective approach aimed at better perceiving one's identity and that of others". They develop the critical sense of students who are prepared to "distinguish between knowledge and belief, the scientific and the symbolic", as well as the construction of spaces for dialogue, in particular in order to counteract "speech of hate and intolerance and to encourage living together." Jewish religious education teachers mainly teach Jewish history and Hebrew.

Religious education programs in secondary education establishments are the subject of a presentation at the annual conference bringing together civil authorities (Rectorate/Académie de Strasbourg et de Nancy) and religious authorities (Bishops, Church presidents and Chief Rabbis).

Cultural and religious awakening (CRE) is a teaching intended for all students in a middle or high school. However, it constitutes an educational method of religious education and is not in principle obligatory since it is provided by religious education teachers within the framework of the resources allocated to this education by the administration. The ECR is most often established at the request of a head of school in technical high schools where religious education no longer exists. The creation of an ECR course takes place at the initiative of a teacher or a team of teachers carrying a project which must be approved by the head of the establishment and the religious authority, the educational council having issued an opinion. The ECR is most often part of the school project, and this at the request of the principal. In this case, it does not require registration like traditional Catholic and Protestant religious education courses.

III.3 The creation of an "Education for Interreligious and Intercultural Dialogue" (EDII) programme

The three eastern departments of France are no exception to the trends observed elsewhere in Europe: secularization of society, loss of influence of religious denominations on populations, religious pluralism, significant decline in religious knowledge, development of fundamentalist, literalist and radical religious currents. Faced with these developments, the expectations of the various players, while converging in substance, each have their own specificities. Pupils' parents want a distanced and non-partisan transmission of religious facts and a good knowledge of other religions, religious authorities emphasize a "lived" approach to religion, taking into account the pluralism of religions and beliefs, while public authorities focus on the creation of social links between pupils of different religions – living and doing together – and a distanced presentation of religion and religious facts.

Religious education under local law must take account of the demands made by these three players, while ensuring – and this is the role of the religious authorities of the statutory religions – that the most representative non-statutory religions, such as Islam and Buddhism, are given a place in this debate.

Religious education under local law has gradually adapted to changes in society. Catechesis classes were abandoned in favor of teaching integrated into the methodology implemented by National Education. Interfaith religion classes (Catholic and Protestant) have been organized for decades in primary schools. "Cultural and religious awakening" (ECR) teaching has been provided for several years in certain secondary schools.

The religious authorities of statutory religions, aware of their responsibilities arising from their particular status within the Republic, decided in 2015 to take a further step and reflect on the creation of religious teaching favoring interreligious and intercultural dimensions. entitled "Teaching in education for interreligious and intercultural dialogue" (EDII). This involves overcoming the deficits in religious knowledge, paying attention to the religious pluralism of our societies, integrating Muslim and Buddhist students and encouraging living and acting together by not separating students according to of their religious affiliation during religion classes.

The Catholic and Protestant faiths, in collaboration with the Jewish faith, conducted a reflection for more than a year.[27] The draft program on interreligious matters for middle and high schools rules out the hypothesis of a religion by religion presentation. It is in fact a teaching program structured around the interreligious dimension of religion. Knowledge of each religion is provided through the prism of this approach taking into account the following elements: beliefs, practices, texts, values, heritage, experiences and communities.

In middle schools, the theme applying to beliefs focuses on their diversity, their divergences and convergences and on the contemporary reality of religious pluralism. Religious practices will be discussed through a contextualized presentation of the main religious festivals and their concrete implementation in the different religions. The different founding texts, their sources, their reading levels will be the subject of comparative studies. The presentation of the values specific to each religion will be broken down by themes such as fraternity, the criteria for just action and the major questions of life. Archaeological and historical traces, the shapes and symbols of great religious monuments, and notable religious personalities will constitute the elements of the heritage course. Teaching on experiences will favor concrete approaches: development of a solidarity project, observation and analysis of religious practices, relationships experienced in a peaceful context. Finally,

27 *Messner*, Les évolutions de l'enseignement religieux en droit local alsacien mosellan, Revue d'Histoire et de philosophie religieuses 2017, n° 97, p. 111–130.

the study of communities will focus on the mechanisms leading to radicalization and on aspects linked to the normative regulation of religious institutions and public institutions with work on the texts organizing life in society. Teachers will highlight the peacemaking potential of different religions.

In high schools, the theme of beliefs will be addressed through the distinction between knowing and believing, the question of believing in a secularized society, activities of a sectarian nature and new religiosities. Practices will be covered through the analysis of rituals, liturgies and religious festivals while courses on founding texts will focus on the context of their writing, the problems linked to their translation and the relationship of believing individuals to the texts. Questions about the links between religious values and republican values, the deconstruction of postures linked to racism and a reflection on the consistency between words and actions will form the content of the teaching on values. The courses on heritage will apply to the relationships between religion, musical arts, cinematographic arts and visual arts while those on experiences will address religion experienced in a radical way, spiritual and mystical experiences and the place of prayer in religious activities. The fight against different discriminations is taught in the course entitled "communities".

The approach initiated by UEPAL and the diocese of Strasbourg was not approved by the authorities of the diocese of Metz. The Bishop of Metz in a press release dated 28 March 2018 declared that:

> The current status offers families the freedom of choice for religious training consistent with their own convictions or the provision of this teaching. Under no circumstances can there be any question of substituting genuine teaching of the Catholic religion for an interreligious course. True dialogue can only be built if everyone is well trained in their own tradition. Restricting ourselves to a comparative analysis of religions can only impoverish the training of young people and run the risk of developing religious syncretism. This would not be respectful of the choice of families, nor of different religious traditions [...]

Finally, the national education administration has expressed reluctance regarding cooperation with unrecognized religions. It notably recalled that in accordance with the jurisprudence of the Constitutional Council "the obligation of the State to provide religious education is limited to only the four religions recognized before the entry into force of the constitution [...] the State cannot therefore, on the basis of local law to finance the teaching of another religion, in particular the Muslim religion in public schools in these departments."[28]

---

28 Question n° O5222, *Journal officiel*, Sénat du 31 aout 2018, p. 2586

Finally, it is recalled that the Council of State requires the State to organize a denominational religious education course and that the organization of an interreligious course deprives this teaching of its denominational character. Such a measure could not be considered legal with regard to the obligations incumbent on the State.

This strict interpretation of constitutional and administrative jurisprudence on the part of the executive calls for at least one remark. The religious authorities of statutory religions have the right to change the content of religious courses in accordance with the principle of freedom of organization of religions. The interreligious dimension of religion courses is not non-denominational in nature.

But following new negotiations between the authorities of statutory religions, the Ministry and the Rector of the academy, the active participation of non-statutory religions, were abolished. The new project submitted to the Rectorate of the Academy of Strasbourg recommends that

> Within the framework of current local law and to accommodate changes in French society, Catholic and Protestant religious authorities are proposing in Alsace a new method of religious education for the secondary. This project is part of respecting the administrative framework of teaching positions identified in one of the three components of local school status: Catholic, Protestant or Jewish. We call this new modality of religious education, courses of Education for Interreligious and Intercultural Dialogue (EDII). It is part of the framework of the common base of knowledge, skills and culture (Decree 2015---372 of 03.31.2015) and extends the objective, critical and non-catechetical approach of religious education [...] This course does not replace the denominational course but could be offered as an extension of the Cultural and Religious Awakening (ECR) modality in high school.

IV. Conclusion

Religious education, the attendance of which is in constant decline throughout France, has great difficulty maintaining itself in schools, middle and high schools, whether in general law or in local law. The first reason for this decline is the secularization of society which leads to a reduction in the number of students but also a difficulty in finding trained teachers. The second reason is linked to the marginal place and the lack of integration of religious education in the French education system. Attempts to organize this teaching, particularly in the local law of Alsatian Moselle religions, have encountered legal obstacles which have the effect of crystallizing fragile achievements. This situation is paradoxical in that it goes against the grain of insistent social demands aimed at developing the religious knowledge of younger generations with a view to promoting religious peace and living together.

Pastoral Care of the Catholic Church in the Armed Forces and Armed Units of the Slovak Republic[1]

VOJTECH VLADÁR

I. Introduction

Special pastoral care was within living memory supposed to be applied especially for the people performing the professions connected with the danger of death. Especially on that account were, according to the preserved historical sources, various types of clergymen or spiritual persons with connection to the metaphysics (druids, oracles etc.) always the firm part of military units. Their task was not only to foretell the favour of gods to gain victory in the forthcoming battle, but also to encourage the soldiers to be brave, pointing out the advantages of laying down their life for homeland and future rewards connected with such a sacrifice at the metaphysical level. These expectations were relevant especially in religions proclaiming the future eternal life in blessedness, whereby this doctrine was from its establishment also the firm part of the Christianity. Even on that account we find in the period of Antiquity several examples pointing out the successive substitution of pagan cult with Christian religion also in this area.

From the times of the Early Middle Ages were the catholic clergymen the common part of campaigns of Christian sovereigns, undertaking frequently not only pastoral, but also military functions. The spiritual care for soldiers was preserved even in the later era, although the status of the Catholic Church in the secular society was gradually weakened. This conclusion is still up-to-date, despite the long period of peace lasting in Europe in principle from the times of the Second World War (1939–1945). Slovak Republic is not the exception within this context, because, after the fall of the socialist regime and dissolution of the Czech and Slovak Federative Republic, its representatives were accommodating not only towards the Catholic Church, but also other churches and religious societies, trying to compensate at least partly the committed injustices. Following the aim to regulate its faculties within the area of pastoral care for soldiers and members of other

---

1 The article is the output of the research project VEGA No. 1/0548/22 entitled "Crisis of Trust and its Roman-Canonical Solutions".

armed forces was in 2002 even contracted the international Treaty between the Slovak Republic and the Holy See on Pastoral Care for Catholic Believers in the Armed Forces and Armed Units of the Slovak Republic that was in 2005 succeeded by the internal Agreement between the Slovak Republic and Registered Churches and Religious Societies on the Performance of Pastoral Services to their Believers in the Armed Forces and Armed Units of the Slovak Republic.

II. Historical Background

As generally known, religion had always its firm place in the battlefields, whereby this fact may be demonstrated even by the sources containing reports on battles from the pre-Christian times.[2] The situation did not change after the establishment of Christianity in the Roman Empire, when for example the *Emperor Constantine the Great* (306–337), according to the well-known legend, defeated in 312 AD under sign of the cross his co-regent *Maxentius* (306–316) in the Battle of the Milvian Bridge in Rome.[3] Even the later the expansion of new religion between the Germanic nations was connected with the fact that Christianity was considered to be the religion of victors.[4] Regarding the period of Middle Ages, the presence of priests alongside with warriors was usual.[5] In addition, then bishops also head the armies and within this context we may mention the well-known Ugrian *Bishop Paul Tomori* († 1526) that participated the famous, though catastrophic for the Kingdom of Hungary, Battle of Mohács (1526). Of course, in the period of Antiquity it is hard to find some institutional form of the spiritual care in the armed forces that was established only in the Modern Period.

---

2 Within this context we may for example mention the provision of the Old Testament referring to the priest inciting the warriors of the Jewish army. Dt 20,2–4.

3 The presence of Christian priests and deacons is moreover evidenced in the military camps of this Emperor. *Pugliese*, La cura castrense: Evoluzione e Natura del Diritto Canonico nell'Ordinamento Statuale, 1943, Torino, p. 5–6.

4 On that account so-called Apostle of Goths, bishop Wulfila († 383) summarized the principles of Christian dogmatic into simple schemes and selected from Gospels several passages related with the morals of power, energy and heroism. Although after this manner he secured success to his missions, on the other hand the Germanic nations typically did not accept Christianity due to the conviction of its truth, but rather for its power. In fact, the acceptance of new religion was determined by the power and greatness of new God that should be manifested especially in the military victories (*fortissimus est deorum, pontentissimus deorum*). See also *Doležal*, Interakcie Gótů a římského imperia ve 3.–5. století n. l. [The Interaction of Goths and Roman Empire in 3.–5. Century AD], 2008, Praha, p. 256 ff.

5 This attitude prevailed especially in the times of Charlemagne (768/800–814). *Viana*, Territorialidad y personalidad en la organización eclesiástica. El caso de los ordinariatos militares, 1992, Pamplona, p. 23–30.

Within this context we may mention that roots of the pastoral care in the Habsburg army reaches in the period of Thirty Years' War (1618–1648), though it obtained the institutional character only in the seventies years of the 18th century, with relation to the military reforms of the *Empress Mary Theresa* (1740/1765–1780). Under its authority the spiritual care was exempted from the competence of diocesan bishops and also the special military ordinariate was established with the consent of the Holy See.[6] Even the majority of later religious reforms found its reflections in the army reforms and for example after publishing of the Edict of Tolerance of 1781 the Evangelical pastors were also included, whereby in 1839 was decided that every soldier is entitled to the spiritual care, regardless of his own confession.[7] Of course, due to the Catholic character of the Habsburg monarchy, it is not surprising that in the army the Catholic clergymen prevailed. At the head of the Catholic military clergy was the apostolic military chaplain, disposing of the Church dignity of a bishop and military rank of major general.[8]

Before the First World War (1914–1918) was allocated to the armycorps of the Austro-Hungarian army military superiors with the rank of lieutenant colonel to whom were subordinated military chaplains with the rank of major, or captain. They provided for pastoral care not only in the individual garrisons, but also in the military hospitals and houses of invalids. Every division had its own main parish priest, whereby at individual regiments served the military spirituals of that domination, to which the majority of squad belonged.[9] Every priest had to fulfil specific conditions to become the military chaplain, that is to say perfect health condition, age of less than forty years and three-year practice of priestly service. Regarding the multi-national composition of the Austro-Hungarian army each of them had to master, in addition to the German language, at least one of the other languages of the nations of the monarchy.[10] Concerning the concrete numbers, in the peace

---

6 *Kumor*, Cirkevné dejiny 6. Novovek. Obdobie absolutizmu a osvietenstva [Church History 6. Modern Times. The Period of Absolutism and Enlightenment], 2003, Levoča, p. 106 ff.

7 However, only confessors of the religions recognized by the state disposed of this right. *Melmuková*, Patent zvaný toleranční [Patent Entitled Toleration], 1999, Praha, p. 16–17 and 28.

8 At the beginning of 20th century the director of military consistory was liable to the apostolic military chaplain, disposing of two representatives with the rank of lieutenant colonel or major. *Žiarovský*, Zabudnutí vojenskí biskupi [Forgotten Military Bishops]. Available at www.postoj.sk/51626/zabudnuti-vojenski-biskupi (accessed 25 July 2025).

9 Moreover, the rule was accepted that in every division should be at disposition one Evangelical spiritual at least. In the navy the spiritual hierarchy consisted of navy superior, to whom navy parish priest (archpriest) and individual navy chaplains were subordinated. Like today, the army rules concerning the organization of the spiritual care were related also to the gendarmerie. *Žiarovský* (note 8).

10 As an ideal was presented the ability of every military chaplain to speak with soldiers commended to him in their own national language. Especially on that account in the Austro-Hungarian army asserted particularly the priests from Galicia, Czechia, Croatia, Transylvania and from Slovakia. Mainly within the context of unwisely enforced Hungarian assimilatory national politics, these rights were not related to the non-Hungarian nations. See also *Grešková* (ed.), Vzťahy štátu a cirkví v Európe.

periods served in the army approximately 160 Catholic military chaplains. To the farther units were to provide for the spiritual care invited also the local secular priests that could work in the mentioned position with the consent of their bishop and after obtaining the authority to perform the function of subsidiary military spiritual administrator. Their number increased especially after the general mobilization related to all of the priests in the recruiting age, when in the war years 1914 to 1918 passed the army approximately 3 300 clergymen. As mentioned in the literature, these numbers turned out to be insufficient and on that account every military chaplain took care for several military units, in common remote from one another also couple of kilometres. Their main duties consisted especially in the celebration of sacraments (primarily the Last Sacrament).[11] Since the military commanders realized that presence of clergyman strengthen the morals of a unit, mentioned found its reflection in their appeals to preach to support the patriotism and martial spirit.[12]

Military spirituals performed their activities also in the army of the First Czechoslovak Republic, whereby the situation did not change in the times of the Second World War, when it was practised in the Slovak army. Some researchers, while analyzing this topic, moreover distinctively distinguish two closely interconnected periods, namely the period from the establishment of the First Slovak Republic, that is to say 14th March 1939, until the appointment of the auxiliary bishop of the Apostolic Administration of Trnava *Michal Buzalka* († 1961) to the vicar of military forces (*vicarious castrensis*) on 4th June 1940; and the period of creation, formation and existence of the Vicariate of Military Forces from June 1940 until the end of war in May 1945, when the Slovak Republic and its army ceased to exist.[13] The first period was characterized especially by the preparatory works leading to the stabilization of new-established Catholic military spiritual service in the army of the Slovak Republic, what found its reflection in taking over of structures according to the mentioned models of the army of the former First Czechoslovak Republic.[14] In

Súčasné otázky a trendy na začiatku 21. storočia [Relationships of State and Churches in Europe. Contemporary Questions and Tendencies at the Beginning of 21st Century], 2010, Bratislava, p. 10.

11 Although mentioned sacrament could be, according to the rules of canon law, celebrated to the soldier in the state of apparent danger of death, for example the amputation of a limb, or state of serious military danger before the battle was not considered to be relevant. Mentioned is nevertheless in defiance with its current celebrating to the people subjectively considering themselves to be seriously ill. See also *Hrdina*, Kanonické právo, 2002, Praha, p. 282.

12 *Žiarovský* (note 8).

13 *Huďa*, Periodizácia existencie katolíckej vojenskej duchovnej služby v slovenskej armáde v rokoch 1939–1945 [Periodization of Existence of the Catholic Military Spiritual Service in the Slovak Army in 1939–1945], Acta Facultatis Theologiae Universitatis Comenianae Bratislaviensis 2/2022, p. 78.

14 As a mater of interest we may mention that even prepared concordat aspiring to improve the relationships between the First Slovak Republic and Holy See, supposed the military spiritual service, reserving the promulgation of relevant regulations to the Holy See. Art. 8. See also *Petranský*, Štát a

the second period then the Vicariate of Military Forces performed its activities.[15] From the contemporary point of view it is more than interesting that impulse to constitute it did not arise from the Church environments, but from military and state spheres.[16] Namely, until the times of its establishment the Catholic spiritual service in the army was performed by competent bishops conferring their powers to the military chaplains in the garrisons falling under their jurisdiction.[17] Except for the regular officers of military service performed their activities also the civil clergymen centralized at so-called auxiliary spiritual administrations.[18] Military spiritual service was performed also in the times of military emergency, when Slovakia alongside with German army entered the campaign against the Soviet Union. The multitude of military spirituals may be illustrated by the fact that ordinaries were trying, by means of repeated requests, to achieve the release of their priests from this service and their return to their parishes.[19] After the Second World War, with reference to the ideological background of new socialist regime, absented the political will to accept the spiritual service in the military structures. This attitude was asserted in 1946 when the pastoral activities in the army ceased to exist *de facto*, whereby this fact was officially confirmed in 1950.[20] Of course, its restoration in the Slovak army was possible only after the fall of mentioned regime (1989) and formation of the independent Slovak Republic (1993), in the concrete in the autumn of 1994.

---

katolícka cirkev na Slovensku 1945–1946 [The State and the Catholic Church in Slovakia 1945–1946], 2001, Nitra, p. 29 ff.

15 See also *Huďa*, Katolícki vojenskí duchovní na východnom a talianskom fronte v rokoch 1941–1945 [Catholic Military Clergymen in the Eastern and Italian Front in 1941–1945], 2021, Bratislava, p. 14 ff.

16 See also *Letz*, V hodine veľkej skúšky [In Hour of a Big Trial], 2007, Trnava, p. 114–115.

17 *Huďa* (note 13), p. 83.

18 The main activities of military clergymen were as follows: organizing of various spiritual, pedagogic and educational activities, providing for various edifying-moral lectures, obligatory administering of so-called military diaries and sending of specific reports. In addition, they usually did not refuse various commissions of military character (with the exception of commanding and supervisory tasks), as far as it was not in conflict with Christian morality, including their assistance to the medical personnel and functions of postal officers etc. Every military chaplain had at disposal his own military servant to assist them while celebrating the liturgy (as ministrants), but also to defend them, since they did not dispose of weapons. Of course, these servants had to be Catholics, whereby only the lowest military ranks were granted to them. See also *Huďa*, Vzťahy katolíckych vojenských duchovných s veliteľmi a vojakmi na východnom fronte v rokoch 1941–1945 [The Relationships between the Catholic Military Clergymen and Commanders and Soldiers in the Eastern Front in 1941–1945], Acta Facultatis Theologiae Universitatis Comenianae Bratislaviensis 1–2/2021, p. 72 ff.

19 *Huďa* (note 13), p. 99.

20 *Pejs*, Vojenští duchovní v poválečné československé armádě (1946–1950) [Military Clergymen in the Postwar Czechoslovak Army (1946–1950)], Historie a vojenství 4/1992, p. 136.

III. Universal Canon Law

As mentioned, clergymen provided for the pastoral care in the armed forces practically from the times of Antiquity. Universal canon law then started to regulate their activities in the Modern Period, namely after the Thirty Years' War. As an ideal was considered to be the creation of special structures with the individual prelate with the corresponding jurisdiction at its head.[21] These premises were accepted even by later instruction of the Sacred Consistorial Congregation entitled *Solemne semper* of 23rd April 1951 that was reflected during the preparatory works to the Second Vatican Council (1962–1965). In those times it was supposed that prepared legislation can not be formulated strictly in formalistic and generalizing way, namely on that account that number of Catholic believers bound with the military service was not the same everywhere. These conclusions manifested especially in the Council document *Christus Dominus* (1966) that emphasized the need of spiritual care for the Catholics in the armed forces with regard to the specific needs of each of them.[22] For that reason only few general rules valid for all the military ordinariates had to be constituted (until then called military vicariates) and this attitude found its reflection also in the valid Code of Canon Law of 1983, which kept in force majority of valid laws, respectively it changed them in slightly way only.[23] Within this context it is necessary to highlight this area is in common regulated by the rules of concordat law that takes precedence as *ius speciale* over the universal *ius generale*.[24] Especially on this background the most optimal solution appeared to supplement the fundamental rules by means of statutes authorized by the Apostolic See for every ordinariate individually. This attitude was reflected also in the legislation of the Pope John Paul II (1978–2005) that regulated this problematic in the Apostolic Constitution *Spiritum militum curae*, promulgated in 1986.

Looking closely into mentioned source, it first and foremost compares the military ordinariates from the legal point of view to the dioceses administered under the authority of individual statute approbated by the Apostolic See. At the head of each is its own ordinary, generally with the dignity of a bishop, nevertheless with all the faculties of the diocesan bishop that is nominated or eventually at least confirmed by the Pope.[25] Their jurisdiction is then characterized as personal, since it is applied towards all of the Catholics belonging to the ordinariate, even in case of being beyond the national borders; common for external and internal forum;

---

21 Innocent X, breve *Cum sicut majestatis*, 26.9.1645 in *Bullarium Romanum* 15.

22 Spirituali militum curae, Praefatio, in: AAS 78/1986, p. 481–486.

23 Can. 569 CIC 1983.

24 Cann. 3 CIC 1983 and 4 CCEO 1990.

25 Cann. 163 and 377 § 1 CIC 1983 and 181 § 2 CCEO 1990. Its importance is emphasized by the request that every military ordinary should be in principle freed from all other pastoral duties. Spirituali militum curae 2 § 3.

independent, but also cumulative with the judicial authority of competent diocesan bishops, because persons coming under the ordinariate remain also believers of given particular church according to their domicile, eventually rite.[26] Concerning presbytery of military ordinariate, its members may come from diocesan and regular priests that could be afforded to the military ordinariate by diocesan bishops, or competent superiors of regular orders.[27] Priests performing their spiritual activities in the ordinariate as chaplains then have the rights and duties of parish priests within the frame of determined boundaries and towards persons entrusted to them.[28] According to the rules of universal law, to the military ordinariate automatically belongs Catholics, which are soldiers, as well as other people serving in the army; their family members, thus wives and children, including those, which reached age of majority, but residing with their parents in the same household, as well as their relatives and service staff residing in the same household; students of military schools or personnel of military hospitals or other similar institutions; Catholics performing the stable services authorized by the commission of military ordinary, or at least with his consent.[29] Every military ordinary shall give report on the condition of his ordinariate to the Apostolic See once in five years, namely according to the form prepared by the competent dicastery.[30]

IV. Particular Slovak Canon Law and State Religious Law

As mentioned, particular canon law is in the analyzed area in the Slovak Republic regulated especially by the Treaty between the Slovak Republic and the Holy See on Pastoral Care for Catholic Believers in the Armed Forces and Armed Units of the Slovak Republic, published on 28th November 2002 under No. 648/2002 Z. z., as an announcement of the Foreign Office of the Slovak Republic. This source was nevertheless supposed by the Article 14 and 15 of the Basic Treaty between the

---

26 Spirituali militum curae 4.

27 Spirituali militum curae 6.

28 Spirituali militum curae 7. According to the rules of universal law, for the believers belonging to the military ordinariate is in the first instance competent diocesan court residing in the curia of the military ordinariate. Appellate court then has to be closely specified in the statute. If an ordinariate has it own court, appellations are sent to the court specified by the military ordinary with the permission of the Apostolic See. Cann. 1438, ° 2 and 1064 § 2 CCEO 1990.

29 Spirituali militum curae 10.

30 Within this context we refer to the Dicastery for Bishops. Praedicate Evangelium, in: AAS 108/2016, p. 1071–1074. Of course, since at the head of each military ordinariate is a person with the dignity, or at least with the faculties of a diocesan bishop, they are also bound with the duty of regular visits *ad limina*. Cann. 399 and 400 §§ 1–2 CIC 1983 and 206 §§ 1–2 and 208 §§ 1–2 CCEO 1990. See also Sacra Congregatio consistorialis, De sacrorum liminum visitatione a vicariis castrensibus peragenda, in: AAS 51/1959, p. 272–274.

Holy See and the Slovak Republic, undersigned on 24th November 2000 in Vatican and promulgated under No. 326/2001 Z. z. as an announcement of the Foreign Office of the Slovak Republic. From the point of non-Catholic registered churches and religious societies, it was followed by the Agreement between the Slovak Republic and Registered Churches and Religious Societies on Pastoral Care for their Believers in the Armed Forces and Armed Units of the Slovak Republic that was published under No. 270/2005 Z. z.[31] Considering the first mentioned, it is preferentially derived from the universal rules of the Apostolic Constitution *Spirituali militum curae*. The overall attitude leading up to the conclusion of mentioned treaties was connected especially with the professionalization of the Slovak army.[32] The main goal of the treaty with the Catholic Church was to set the principles concerning its organization and realization of the spiritual care, in accordance with canon law and the law and order of the Slovak Republic in the armed forces and armed units of the Slovak Republic.[33] Under its authority the Catholic Church, and later also other contractual registered churches and religious societies, was able to provide for the spiritual care in the armed forces and armed units of the Slovak Republic, as well as in the police forces, detention centres and prisons.[34]

---

31 Contracting parties were in this case following churches and religious societies: the Evangelical Church of the Augsburg Confession in Slovakia; the Reformed Christian Church in Slovakia; the Orthodox Church in Slovakia, Evangelical Methodist Church, Slovak Province; the Unity of the Brethren Baptists in Slovakia; the Church of the Brethren in the Slovak Republic; the Seventh-day Adventist Church, Slovak Congregation; the Apostolic Church in Slovakia; the Central Union of Jewish Religious Communities in the Slovak Republic; the Old-Catholic Church in Slovakia and the Czechoslovak Hussite Church in Slovakia. Dohoda medzi Slovenskou republikou a registrovanými cirkvami a náboženskými spoločnosťami o výkone pastoračnej služby ich veriacim v ozbrojených silách a ozbrojených zboroch Slovenskej republiky publikovaná pod č. 270/2005 Z. z. [Agreement between the Slovak Republic and Registered Churches and Religious Societies on Pastoral Care for their Believers in the Armed Forces and Armed Units of the Slovak Republic, published in the Collection of Laws under No. 270/2005].

32 These procedures started in 1998 and were completed in 2005. Zákon č. 370/1997 Z. z. o vojenskej službe a zákon č. 346/2005 Z. z. o štátnej službe profesionálnych vojakov ozbrojených síl Slovenskej republiky [Law on State Service of Professional Soldiers of the Armed Forces of the Slovak Republic, published in the Collection of Laws under No. 370/1997].

33 From the secular point of view, its provisions were exercised under the authority of the Resolution of the Government of the Slovak Republic. Uznesenie vlády Slovenskej republiky č. 1115/2003 k návrhu opatrení na realizáciu Zmluvy medzi SR a Svätou stolicou o duchovnej službe katolíckym veriacim v ozbrojených silách a ozbrojených zboroch [Resolution of the Government of the Slovak Republic No. 1115/2003 to the Proposal of Provisions for the Realization of the Treaty between the Slovak Republic and the Holy See on Pastoral Care for Catholic Believers in the Armed Forces and Armed Units].

34 To the date of conclusion of this treaty the Catholic Church performed its activities in the Department of Defence of the Slovak Republic for eight years, in the Corps of prison and court guard for six years, but not in the Department of Home Affairs and in the Police forces. From those times it started to provide for the pastoral care in the structures of the armed forces and armed units of the Slovak Republic, Police forces, Corps of prison and court guard, Railroad police, as well as for the persons deprived of liberty by the decision of state body. Zmluva medzi Slovenskou republikou a Svätou

From the Catholic Church point of view was, within the context of the universal canon law and mentioned Treaty, canonically constituted (by the bull *Spiritualem progressionem*) in the army of the Slovak Republic on 1st March 2003 at the level of diocese the individual Military Ordinariate of Slovakia residing in Bratislava. Alongside with the canon-law subjectivity, it is recognized also by legal regulations of the Slovak Republic, in the concrete as a non-profit organization in competence of the Department of Defence.[35] It represents the highest Church office for managing of spiritual care provided for the Catholic believers in the armed forces and armed units, as well as to the persons deprived of liberty by the decision of state body.[36] At its head was in the same year by the Holy See, that is the only one exclusively competent to such an act, nominated the Bishop Mons. František Rábek, remaining in this position up to now. In accordance with the Apostolic Constitution *Spirituali militum curae* is the canon-law jurisdiction of the Ordinary defined as personal, proper, own and cumulative with the authority of local ordinary.[37] Under his authority then belongs following Catholics: members and employees

---

stolicou o duchovnej službe katolíckym veriacim v ozbrojených silách a zboroch Slovenskej republiky, publikovaná 28. novembra 2002 pod č. 648/2002 Z. z. ako oznámenie ministerstva zahraničných vecí Slovenskej republiky, úvod [Treaty between the Slovak Republic and the Holy See on Pastoral Care for Catholic Believers in the Armed Forces and Armed Units of the Slovak Republic, published as an Announcement of the Foreign Office of the Slovak Republic in the Collection of Laws on 28th November 2002 under No. 648/2002, Preface]. The Statute of the ordinariate mentions also the performance of these activities in the Slovak information service (SIS), Fire and rescue corps, Mountain rescue service and Customs administrations. Štatút ordinariátu ozbrojených síl a ozbrojených zborov [Statute of the Military Ordinariate of Slovakia] 1,5,1.

35 Of course, the Ordinariate, as well as all the parishes constituted by the Ordinary are considered to be the corporate entities not only according to canon law but are also registered by the Ministry of Culture of the Slovak Republic. Synoda Ordinariátu ozbrojených síl a ozbrojených zborov Slovenskej republiky [Synod of the Military Ordinariate of Slovakia] § 66. Available at www.ordinariat.sk/dokumenty-synoda/ (accessed 25 July 2025).

36 Zmluva (note 34), 1,1–2. Cathedral Church of the Military Ordinariate of Slovakia is the Church of Saint Sebastian in Bratislava – Krasňany, whereas its patron saint is Saint Sebastian. Štatút ordinariátu ozbrojených síl a ozbrojených zborov [Statute of the Military Ordinariate of Slovakia] 1,2,3 and 1,7. With reference to the other registered churches and religious societies, they constituted, by means of the Ecumenical Council of Churches in the Slovak Republic, the Centre of the Ecumenical Pastoral Service for the Pastoral Care to their Believers in the Armed Forces and Armed Units and to the Persons Deprived of Liberty by the Decision of State Body. Dohoda medzi Slovenskou republikou a registrovanými cirkvami a náboženskými spoločnosťami o výkone pastoračnej služby ich veriacim v ozbrojených silách a ozbrojených zboroch Slovenskej republiky [Agreement between the Slovak Republic and Registered Churches and Religious Societies on the Performance of Pastoral Services to their Believers in the Armed Forces and Armed Units of the Slovak Republic] 1,1.

37 Zmluva (note 34), 2,3. At the head of the Centre of the Ecumenical Pastoral Service is then the general priest nominated by the Ecumenical Council of Churches, responsible for all the activities in the area of pastoral service. Dohoda medzi Slovenskou republikou a registrovanými cirkvami a náboženskými spoločnosťami o výkone pastoračnej služby ich veriacim v ozbrojených silách a ozbrojených zboroch Slovenskej republiky [Agreement between the Slovak Republic and Registered Churches and Religious Societies on the Performance of Pastoral Services to their Believers in the Armed Forces and Armed Units of the Slovak Republic] 2.

of the armed forces and armed units, including the employees of the competent bodies of state administration performing their services there; their family members, namely spouses, children (including those, which reached age of majority, residing with their parents in the same household), as well as their relatives residing with them in the common household; students of schools of armed forces and armed units, patients and personnel of health care and social institutions belonging under the competent bodies of the state administration; the Catholic believers appointed or approved by the Ordinary into the permanent service on behalf of Ordinariate; persons in detention, imprisoned, respectively persons detained or secured.[38] To the ordinary are then in his activities helpful general vicar, other vicars, priests and deacons, which are appointed by him.[39] Diocesan bishops and major superiors of the institutes of consecrated life and societies of apostolic life are moreover appealed to release for the needs of Ordinariate adequate number of clergymen, whereas diocesan clergymen may be incardinated into it too.[40] Ordinary may also oblige, with consent of diocesan bishops or mentioned major superiors, their clergymen with temporal or occasional duties in the Ordinariate.[41] The Treaty then constitutes that spiritual service and performing of religious rites is considered to be the part of the performance of service of priests and deacons of the Ordinariate.[42] Distinctively is then regarded potential penalizing of clergymen, namely from the point of view of canon law, as well as secular law. Under these circumstances in case of non-canonical punishment the superior from the armed forces or armed units should penalize the clergyman after previous arrangement with the Ordinary. In case of penalizing by the Ordinary, his only duty consists in notification of the secular superior of clergyman to make proper arrangements.[43] With reference to the financial matters, the Slovak Republic provides for the clergymen of the Ordinariate, as well as for the residence of the Ordinariate, church, its curia and adequate areas intended for the Divine services.[44] The Treaty at the

---

38 Zmluva (note 34), 3.

39 Zmluva (note 34), 4.

40 As a mater of interest we may mention that other registered churches and religious societies perform their activities in the area of pastoral care by the medium of clergymen and deacons proposing it to the extent of their competencies and without any reference to their confession. Of course, religious rites are celebrated according to their internal regulations. Dohoda medzi Slovenskou republikou a registrovanými cirkvami a náboženskými spoločnosťami o výkone pastoračnej služby ich veriacim v ozbrojených silách a ozbrojených zboroch Slovenskej republiky [Agreement between the Slovak Republic and Registered Churches and Religious Societies on the Performance of Pastoral Services to their Believers in the Armed Forces and Armed Units of the Slovak Republic] 9,1–2.

41 Zmluva (note 34), 5. With reference to the priests and deacons permanently delegated to the spiritual services in the Ordinariate, they dispose of the rights and duties of the diocesan priests and deacons. Zmluva (note 34), 7.

42 Zmluva (note 34), 8.

43 Zmluva (note 34), 9.

44 Zmluva (note 34), 10.

same time supposes more detailed elaboration of these rules in the Statute of the Military Ordinariate of Slovakia that was promulgated in time of its constitution in 2003.[45]

Examining mentioned Statute in more detail, it is at first sight evident that majority of its provisions is derived from the analyzed sources and reproduces its text. Of course, several rules are elaborated in more detail. Within this context we may mention for example the regulation that Ordinary may constitute in the armed forces and armed units also personal parishes and spiritual administrations that could acquire the legal personality, namely according to the rules of canon law, as well as secular law. In addition, the military units in case of vacancy or obstructing of office or in the absence of Ordinary, vicar general or priests of the Ordinariate, are subject to the authority of local ordinaries and parish priests that may under these circumstances act on the basis of their own law.[46] Concerning the status of the Ordinary, he is the proper member of the Conference of Slovak Bishops and he attends their sessions and meetings regularly.[47] Other articles deal especially with the curia of the Ordinariate that consists of vicar general, Episcopal vicar, chancellor and other personnel.[48] Ordinary may at the same time appoint the Episcopal vicars including other Episcopal vicars with specific responsibilities.[49] Considering the financing of the curia, it is in the concrete provided by the Department of Defence of the Slovak Republic.[50] In the Ordinariate is also constituted the Episcopal Council consisting of vicar general and Episcopal vicars, as well as Presbytery Council comprising of the priests of the presbytery of the Ordinariate.[51] Distinct emphasis is then put on the fact that clergymen of the Ordinariate

---

45 Also the Centre of the Ecumenical Pastoral Service disposes of its own statute, prepared by the general priest and approved by the participating churches and religious societies. Dohoda medzi Slovenskou republikou a registrovanými cirkvami a náboženskými spoločnosťami o výkone pastoračnej služby ich veriacim v ozbrojených silách a ozbrojených zboroch Slovenskej republiky [Agreement between the Slovak Republic and Registered Churches and Religious Societies on the Performance of Pastoral Services to their Believers in the Armed Forces and Armed Units of the Slovak Republic] 1,3.

46 Štatút ordinariátu ozbrojených síl a ozbrojených zborov [Statute of the Military Ordinariate of Slovakia] 1,6,3.

47 Štatút ordinariátu ozbrojených síl a ozbrojených zborov [Statute of the Military Ordinariate of Slovakia] 2,9.

48 Štatút ordinariátu ozbrojených síl a ozbrojených zborov [Statute of the Military Ordinariate of Slovakia] 3,12.

49 Štatút ordinariátu ozbrojených síl a ozbrojených zborov [Statute of the Military Ordinariate of Slovakia] 3,14, 1–2.

50 Štatút ordinariátu ozbrojených síl a ozbrojených zborov [Statute of the Military Ordinariate of Slovakia] 3,18.

51 From the members of the Presbytery Council is moreover constituted the College of Consultors. The functions of both mentioned bodies are only advisory and are related especially to the orientation of the spiritual service of the Ordinariate and its coordination. Similar tasks are provided also by the Pastoral Council that examines the relevant pastoral activities. Economic Council than administers

can not be commissioned with tasks incompatible with their service.[52] The priests of the Ordinariate are appointed by the Ordinary to the office of military, police or prison chaplains, whereby the chaplain to which the personal parish or spiritual administration was committed disposes in principle of the rights and duties of the territorial parish priest.[53] Concerning the court jurisdiction, in the first instance is competent the Metropolitan Tribunal of Bratislava and in the second the Archdiocesan Tribunal of Trnava.[54]

Previous information is available also in other sources of law, or non-legal sources, especially in the provisions of the Synod of the Military Ordinariate of Slovakia (2014–2017), or from the older document entitled "The Conception of Development of the Spiritual Service in the Armed Forces of the Slovak Republic" (2005). There we may find for example the regulation that whereas in the armed forces and armed units of the Slovak Republic represents the supreme body responsible for the spiritual service to the Catholic believers the Ordinariate itself, the specific body for the armed forces represents the Vicariate of the Ordinariate for the Armed Forces. In addition, at the individual ministries perform their activities the Vicariate of the Ordinariate for the Department of Home Affairs and Vicariate of the Ordinariate for the Department of Justice.[55] Within this context we may mention also the Vicariate of the Corps of Prison and Court Guard.[56] Vicariate of the Ordinary for the Armed Forces is then organizationally affiliated to the General Staff of the Armed Forces of the Slovak Republic.[57] Within the armed forces is then the Ordinariate structured into deanships situated at the headquarters of Ground Forces, Air Units, Forces of Training and Support and at the National Academy of Defence of Marshal *Andrej Hadik*.[58] The main entity of the Ordinariate is then parish committed to the clergyman, acting as a dean or chaplain,

---

the common fund and deals with economical and material matters. Štatút ordinariátu ozbrojených síl a ozbrojených zborov [Statute of the Military Ordinariate of Slovakia] 4,19–21.

52 For example, clergymen may not dispose of service weapon, to bear or use it. Štatút ordinariátu ozbrojených síl a ozbrojených zborov [Statute of the Military Ordinariate of Slovakia] 5,27,3–4.

53 Of course, also the authority of chaplain is personal and cumulates with the authority of territorial parish priest. On that account, every believer belonging to the Ordinariate may choose the cleric to celebrate the sacraments. Štatút ordinariátu ozbrojených síl a ozbrojených zborov [Statute of the Military Ordinariate of Slovakia] 5,29.

54 Štatút ordinariátu ozbrojených síl a ozbrojených zborov [Statute of the Military Ordinariate of Slovakia] 7,34–35.

55 Synoda Ordinariátu ozbrojených síl a ozbrojených zborov Slovenskej republiky [Synod of the Military Ordinariate of Slovakia] § 65.

56 Ministerstvo obrany Slovenskej republiky, Koncepcia rozvoja duchovnej služby v ozbrojených silách [Department of Defence of the Slovak Republic, The Conception of Development of the Spiritual Service in the Armed Forces] 3.1.1.

57 Ministerstvo obrany Slovenskej republiky, Koncepcia (note 56), 3.2.6.

58 Ministerstvo obrany Slovenskej republiky, Koncepcia (note 56), 3.2.7.

like its regular spiritual pastor. Every one of them has also its own Parish Council that supports the clergyman while realizing his pastoral activities.[59]

Ordinary may appoint the clergymen of the Ordinariate to the Church offices, according to the provisions of canon law, regardless of the rank conceded to them according to the regulations of the Slovak Republic.[60] Number of clergymen is then defined relatively, in conformity with the statistics of religiousness and real needs of the armed forces, in principle in such way that one military clergyman could provide for spiritual care approximately for 1 000 soldiers of the Army of the Slovak Republic. The main condition for their admission is then, according to the legal regulations of the Slovak Republic, sexennial practice in the civil pastoral care and to not exec the age-limit of 45 years. Moreover, every clergyman has to dispose of consent of his Church superior to join the armed forces and of mandate of the Conference of the Slovak Bishops or the Ecumenical Council of Churches in the Slovak Republic.[61] Concerning their contact with their Catholic superiors, every priest of the Ordinariate has to visit the Ordinary at least once a year, whereby the priests not incardinated into the Ordinariate have the same duty in relation to their bishop or religious superior.[62]

Of course, all the pastoral care of the clergymen of the Ordinariate is exclusively under the control of the Ordinariate and Centre of the Ecumenical Pastoral Service, and from the Catholic point of view administered by the Ordinary, respectively general priest. Priests and deacons of the Ordinariate may then perform their spiritual activities according to the relevant liturgical and canon-law regulations.[63] With reference to the activities of the clergymen, they may collaborate on the educational-pedagogical procedures to strengthen the discipline, morality in extreme conditions (especially at war), to protect the public order and justice, as well as while to eliminate the consequences of natural calamities.[64] Of course, the basic activities are organized in the time of service only by the courtesy of superior commander, as far as they do not impede the performance of duties, or in the

---

59 Ministerstvo obrany Slovenskej republiky, Koncepcia (note 56), 3.2.12.

60 Ministerstvo obrany Slovenskej republiky, Koncepcia (note 56), 3.3.4. Of course, to the ranks of the military officers are clergymen of the Ordinariate appointed or promoted under authority of the legal regulations of the Slovak Republic. § 38, ods. 1, písm. d) Zákona č. 346/2005 Z. z. o štátnej službe profesionálnych vojakov v Ozbrojených silách Slovenskej republiky [Law on State Service of Professional Soldiers of the Armed Forces of the Slovak Republic, published in the Collection of Laws under No. 346/2005]. Within this context, following ranks come into account: lieutenant, first lieutenant, captain, major, lieutenant colonel and colonel. Ministerstvo obrany Slovenskej republiky, Koncepcia (note 56), 3.4.8.

61 Ministerstvo obrany Slovenskej republiky, Koncepcia (note 56), 2.2.3.

62 Synoda Ordinariátu ozbrojených síl a ozbrojených zborov Slovenskej republiky [Synod of the Military Ordinariate of Slovakia] §§ 40 and 43.

63 Ministerstvo obrany Slovenskej republiky, Koncepcia (note 56), 3.1.5.

64 Ministerstvo obrany Slovenskej republiky, Koncepcia (note 56), 2.1.4.

non-work time.[65] Especially in connection with the professionalization of the Slovak army the focus of activities of the military clergymen towards the soldiers and their family members was essentially broadened from the military units and institutions beyond the area of the armed forces and to their free time.[66] The dangers of profession of the military clergymen is evident mainly from the statement that in state of emergency they should perform their activities in the units situated in the forward edge of the line of the clash, conflict or intervention, as near as possible to the epicentre of the calamity or the cross fire.[67] In addition, they should continue with their spiritual service also in the case of their capture, namely on behalf of the war prisoners.[68] With reference to the maintenance and supply, they have at dispose (at the expenses of the Slovak Republic) the liturgical clothing, necessary objects and tools, furnished offices including the pastoral rooms. Of course, they have also at disposal the accommodation, namely in the military guesthouses, eventually the government quarters, which are in common allocated to them.[69]

The information on regular activities of the Military Ordinariate of Slovakia is to be found especially on the relatively regularly actualized web page.[70] It reveals for example the fact that for the believers integrated into the Ordinariate the Ordinary publishes regularly his pastoral letters, organizes various types of pilgrim excursions (for example to Rome to see the Holy Father), military pedestrian pilgrimages, pilgrimages of sentenced people with their priests, spiritual revivals and spiritual exercises including various types of liturgical celebrations. In addition the Stations of the Cross are realized in the areas of the prisons or various types of ecumenical Divine services are celebrated. Ordinariate is also behind various types of charitable activities, consisting for example of organizing of collections of gifts for the needs of needy ones or disease-riddens (especially soldiers). Distinct accent is then put on the prevention that manifests for example in the lectures of cured addicts etc. The Ordinary put distinctive emphasis especially on the communication with his priests, as well as with his believers, and this is apparent from his frequent meetings with them, not only in Slovakia (especially within the framework of pastoral visits), but also abroad (for example by means of visits of members of the armed forces participating in the foreign missions). The Ordinary himself or

---

65 Ministerstvo obrany Slovenskej republiky, Koncepcia (note 56), 5.0.5.
66 Ministerstvo obrany Slovenskej republiky, Koncepcia (note 56), 2.3.4.
67 Ministerstvo obrany Slovenskej republiky, Koncepcia (note 56), 2.1.5.
68 Ženevský dohovor o zaobchádzaní s vojnovými zajatcami [Geneva Convention on Prisoners of War] 33.
69 Ministerstvo obrany Slovenskej republiky, Koncepcia (note 56), 2.2.5.
70 We refer to the web page www.ordinariat.sk. All the more interesting is the section "Links", introducing the official web pages of the Ordinariates from around the world, including other Catholic web pages relating to the activities of the Ordinariate. https://www.ordinariat.sk/linky/ (accessed 25 July 2025).

his clergymen also attends several international conferences, meetings with other military ordinaries and clergymen operating in the ordinariates of other countries (for example the meeting of chaplains of Visegrád Group) etc. We may also mention frequent and often repeating events realized by means of the clergymen of the Ordinariate in the form of music events in the prison parishes or in the prison hospitals. In addition, we may mention various expositions of photographs or pictures, various types of sport events (football tournaments or Christmas races etc.), parish balls, various festivals of Christian theatre and many other types of social events (for example on the occasion of anniversary of constitution of the Ordinariate). For the children of the soldiers and employees of the Department of Defence are for example regularly organized the summer camps. Moreover, very often are realized also reverent acts and recollections of killed soldiers (for example in Dukla) etc. In addition, alongside with the Ordinariate operates in the armed forces and armed units also the Civil Union of the Community of Catholic Believers in the Armed Forces and Armed Units of the Slovak Republic that unites the Catholic believers accepting the activities of this union in the field of lay apostolate and participating in it.[71]

V. Conclusion

As evident from previous commentary, the Catholic Church had its place in the army structures practically from the times of foundation of Christianity as a new religion in the Roman Empire, even though its formal institutionalization was realized in the 17th century only. From those times it officially performed their activities in the armies, whereas the Catholic clergymen with appropriate military ranks were considered to be its important and essential part. As testify well-preserved sources, the military chaplains maintained more than serious attitude to their duties and struggled hard to perform the pastoral care in best possible way. On that account it would not be correct to imagine them in the portraits of the book of

---

71 Its main goal consists in assistance to the Ordinary and to the clergymen of the Ordinariate at their pastoral care, in realization of the social and charitable activities, in accordance with the social doctrine of the Catholic Church, in cooperation with other Christian societies (at the ecumenical level) etc. Stanovy Spoločenstva katolíckych veriacich v ozbrojených silách a ozbrojených zboroch Slovenskej republiky [Statutes of the Civil Union of the Community of Catholic Believers in the Armed Forces and Armed Units of the Slovak Republic] 1,3 and 2,1–9. See also Synoda Ordinariátu ozbrojených síl a ozbrojených zborov Slovenskej republiky [Synod of the Military Ordinariate of Slovakia] §§ 111 ff. General expectations from the lay members of the Ordinariate may be mentioned by means of following examples: service of lectors, singing, organizing and participating in processions, prayer meetings of mothers, fathers, fiancés, husbands, families, young people, children, visits of the old and sick and care for them etc. Synoda Ordinariátu ozbrojených síl a ozbrojených zborov Slovenskej republiky [Synod of the Military Ordinariate of Slovakia] § 120.

Jaroslav Hašek († 1923), respectively the movie made according to its proposition, entitled "The Good Soldier Švejk" (in the original "Osudy dobrého vojáka Švejka za světové války"), where the military chaplain Katz was presented as a notorious drunkard and military chaplain Lacina as a glutton, bearing only his belly in mind. Several records from the time of the First World War for example describe how soldiers often instituted improvised field chapels and military chaplains in common celebrated the Holy Masses right in the trenches, when as an altar served few hollow ammunition containers and instead of candlesticks were used the rifle bayonets, where the altar candles were put. After all, the war horrors indeed corresponded with the traditional military proverb, according to which all the soldier in the first line are believers. When the military chaplains were appealed to the controversial sermons to support the patriotism and martial spirit, they seek to point out the war evils as a punishment of God for mankind for its immorality and blasphemy.[72] Also the Second World War testified that relationships between the divisional commanders and Catholic military chaplains were usually more than correct and casual officers convinced themselves they could rely on them not only in the spiritual matters, but in almost everything related to the life in front and military discipline. Even the soldiers did not consider them to be some kind of strange element but were confident they are one of them.[73] Despite considerable long period of peace in Europe, the Catholic Church henceforth reflected the particularities of military spiritual administration that were continually broadened practically in all the armed forces and armed units of the individual countries. During the last few decades these procedures were regulated by the canon-law foundations of the Apostolic Constitution of John Paul II *Spirituali militum curae*, reflecting among other things also the conclusions of the Second Vatican Council. Right in this source is also emphasized the historically verified truth that soldiers, as an individual social class, need, because of their individual life conditions, the concrete and specific form of spiritual care.[74]

---

72 *Žiarovský* (note 8).

73 *Huďa*, Vzťahy katolíckych vojenských duchovných s veliteľmi a vojakmi na východnom fronte v rokoch 1941–1945 [The Relationships between the Catholic Military Clergymen and Commanders and Soldiers in the Eastern Front in 1941–1945], Acta Facultatis Theologiae Universitatis Comenianae Bratislaviensis 1–2/2021, p. 89.

74 Spirituali militum curae, Praefatio.

Chaplaincy in England[1]

MARK HILL KC

I. Introduction

Once narrow in their scope, chaplaincies now encompass a broader range of faiths and beliefs than ever before. With the number of Muslims increasing in England and the diversity of Christian denominations in the UK, chaplains cater to a wider variety of needs. In modern times, chaplaincy constitutes "a position held by a minister of religion within an organization or institution in order to provide spiritual services to its members or inmates". There are three primary pillars to chaplaincy: (1) that "the organization is to some extent a restricted community, whose members would otherwise be unable to access the services normally offered by a religious body to the general public"; (2) "the organization may embrace a distinctive cross-section of the public who warrant a specific type of spiritual ministry"; and (3) "chaplaincies offer the possibility of an independent presence in what are often hierarchical contexts, acting both as bridge-builders and whistle-blowers."

Today, Church of England chaplains have an accredited position by the Professional Standards of Authority.[2] The State or other employer institutions generally engage chaplains as opposed to the religious institution itself. Moreover, "as a matter of individual religious right they are required by the need of the individual to access spiritual advice and assistance even when confined or constrained in some way."[3]

---

1 This paper is an updated version of *Hill*, Chaplaincy Services in Public Institutions in England: History, Law and Practice, published in *Tretera/Horák (eds.)*, Spiritual Care in Public Institutions in Europe, 2019, Berlin, p. 21–38.

2 www.churchofengland.org/about/leadership-and-governance/national-church-institutions/church-england-central-services-2 (accessed 25 July 2025).

3 *Rivers*, The Law of Organized Religions: Between Establishment and Secularism, 2011, Oxford, p. 207; see also *Swift*, Hospital Chaplaincy in the Twenty-First Century: The Crisis of Spiritual Care on the National Health Service, 2009, Farnham, p. 154.

II. Legal framework

Statute, secondary legislation, common law and custom form the basis of chaplaincy law. "Soft law" or quasi-legislation – informal administrative rules in the form, typically, of guidance, or codes of practice – also regulates chaplaincy practice. In modern terms, chaplaincy has three aspects: the right of religious organisations to undertake its ministrations, the right of individuals to receive (or reject) them and the corresponding duty of the state to accommodate their free exercise. Chaplains generally have the status of employees under civil law.[4] However, they may also have to be authorized to function by the relevant religious body to which they belong or with which they are associated. Thus, as a general principle applicable to most chaplaincies, the religious community will nominate the candidate. The institution in which the ministry is performed will appoint the chaplain and will be responsible for remuneration. The host institution takes responsibility for any spiritual space within the institution, such as a chapel or prayer room.

III. Chaplaincy in Public Institutions

III.1 The Armed Forces

Military chaplaincy derives from common law rather as opposed to statute. The Secretary of State may "appoint from time to time any army chaplain to perform the functions of an army chaplain in any [...] extra-parochial district," found in the Army Chaplains Act 1868, s. 6.[5] Chaplaincy exercise is a matter of military law, as currently set out in the King's Regulations (KRs) for the three services: army, navy, and air force (RAF).[6]

Commissioned chaplains are drawn from the list of eligible denominations endorsed by the United Navy, Army and Air Force Board and maintained by the Ministry of Defence: the Anglican, Roman Catholic, Presbyterian, Congregational, Baptist and Methodist Churches, the United Reformed Church, the Church of Scotland, the Assemblies of God, the Elim Pentecostal Church and the Salvation Army. A certain provision includes room for five chaplains from other faith groups – Jewish, Sikh, Hindu, Muslim and Buddhist – all of whom operate across all three services. The Secretary of State for Defence appoints chaplains on the

---

4 This is addressed more fully below.

5 This was extended to the Royal Air Force by SR & O 1918/548 (Rev I p. 896: 1948 I p. 50). For the current status of Army chaplains see *Bailey*, Legal Regulation of the Appointment, Ministry and Episcopal Oversight of Army Chaplains, unpublished LLM dissertation, University of Wales, 1999.

6 For a detailed discussion see *Rivers*, (note 3), p. 208–213.

recommendation of the appropriate Chaplain General following nomination by an accredited representative of the religious organisation concerned.

Notably, some chaplains hold military rank. In the Army, the RAF Chaplain-in-Chief ranks as an air vice-marshal. Conversely, Royal Navy chaplains hold no rank at all. The Explanatory Note to Regulation 3 of the Armed Forces (Naval Chaplains) Regulations 2009 states outlines the following:

> A naval chaplain is commissioned as such, and is not an officer [...] Although subject to service law, a naval chaplain has no rank, and is therefore outranked by no-one [...] Conversely, a naval chaplain outranks no-one [...].

The overall position of chaplaincy comes from KR J837 (*General – Observance of Religion*):

> (1) Christian Chaplains are commissioned [...] to provide for the spiritual wellbeing, pastoral care and moral teaching and guidance of Service personnel and their families, regardless of faith or profession of no faith. They are to be given every support in the fulfilment of their ministry. They are not to be required to perform executive or operational duties save those proper to their profession. When a commissioned Chaplain cannot be made available, civilian Christian clerics of the appropriate denomination may be appointed Officiating Chaplains to the Military.
> (2) The reverent observance of religion in the Armed Forces is of the highest importance. It is the duty of all concerned to make adequate provision for the spiritual and moral needs of all personnel and dependants.

Under KR 114(1), RAF chaplains hold relative rank "solely for the purpose of defining status as regards precedence, discipline and administration [...] They are not, by virtue of that rank, eligible to exercise any executive command, or claim any advantage as regards emoluments (effective or non-effective)". Questions about appointment, status, and duties are further outlined in KRs 839–841.

KR 842 delineates the rules of worship and religious holidays:

> (1) In the light of local circumstances, Christian worship is to be arranged within Service churches or, if necessary, at convenient civilian churches, at suitable times [...] on Sundays, Good Friday and Christmas Day to permit the greatest possible number of personnel to attend. Week-day services are also to be arranged as convenient. Similarly, adherents of the five Recognised World Faiths other than Christian[7] should be

7 Judaism, Sikhism, Hinduism, Islam, and Buddhism.

> permitted to make their religious observances on the days and at the times prescribed by their faith [...]

For nomination purposes, the accredited representative in the Church of England is the bishop; in the Church of Scotland, it is the Committee on Chaplaincy to HM Forces; in the Methodist Church it is the Royal Navy, Army and Royal Air Force Board; in the Catholic Church it is the sending bishop, through the Catholic bishop to the Forces.[8]

Each religious organization maintains communication with their chaplains distinctly.[9] While Church of England chaplains leave their diocesan and then come under the Bishop to the Forces, Church of Scotland chaplains remain on the role of a Presbytery.[10]

The duties of chaplains and officiating clergymen in the Army are regulated by the King's Regulations for the Army 1961.[11] Chaplains, with the exception of Catholic chaplains, come under the Chaplain General in all professional matters. The Principal Roman Catholic Chaplain regulates the chaplains in the Army. It is either through the instructions from the Chaplain General or the Principal Roman Catholic Chaplain that chaplains are posted to units or establishments.[12]

The King's Regulations for the Royal Air Force 1964 outline the duties of chaplains for the Royal Air Force.[13] The duties of chaplains in the Royal Navy are stated in the King's Regulations for the Royal Navy 1967.[14]

III.2 The National Health Service

The NHS has always welcomed chaplains since its inception in 1948,[15] when the Ministry of Health declared that hospitals "should give special attention to provide for the spiritual needs of both patients and staff" and that management committees "should appoint a chaplain – or chaplains from more than one denomination – for every hospital for which they are responsible."[16] In Scotland, Circular

8 *Bailey*, (note 5), p. 16.
9 *Bailey*, (note 5), p. 19.
10 Act VII 1942 and Act VI 1947 of the General Assembly.
11 See paras J1432-J1442.
12 Queen's Regulations for the Army 1961, para. JF.274.
13 See para. 100.
14 See Ch. 44.
15 St Bartholomew's Hospital, for example, was founded by Rahere together with the Priory of St Bartholomew in 1123: the two institutions did not become completely separate until 1420 – and the parish church of St Bartholomew the Less is located within the hospital precincts.
16 Ministry of Health Circular HMC (48) 62 (1948), quoted in *Johnson*, Managing Chaplaincy Service Delivery Scottish Journal of Healthcare Chaplaincy 2003, vol. 6 (1), p. 33.

RHB(S) 1951/12, "Religious services and appointment of chaplains", expressed similar sentiments. The NHS Trusts in England nor Health Boards in Scotland provide chaplaincy services by way of contract. Under the NHS England Standard Contract 2014/15, "The Provider must take account of the spiritual, religious, pastoral and cultural needs of Service Users and must liaise with the relevant authorities as appropriate in each case."[17] Currently, the Scots chaplaincy is governed by the Scottish Government's 2009 guidance, *Spiritual Care & Chaplaincy*. The covering letter reminds the Health Board Chief Executives of three things: that they should appoint a senior lead manager for spiritual care, that their Board's spiritual care policy should be updated in light of the guidance and local need, and that they should provide a round-the-clock service.

The provision of spiritual care for patients and staff in hospitals is governed by State quasi-legislation and is regulated by health service guidelines.[18] For example, *Religion or Belief: A practical guide for the NHS* (2009) "sets out how equality issues in religion or belief relate to the principles that underpin our health objectives."

In the event that the NHS does not deliver adequate chaplaincy purposes, the health service ombudsman has the right to investigate such matters. Additionally, there exists the Network for Pastoral, Spiritual, and Religious Care in Health support group,[19] and the European Network of Health Care Chaplaincy which has issued Standards for Health Care Chaplaincy in Europe (2002).[20]

In 2023, the NHS England provided non-statutory guidance on chaplaincy in its published guidelines.[21]

III.3 Prisons

Under section 7(1) of the Prisons Act 1952 every prison in England and Wales should have "[…] a governor, a chaplain and a medical officer"; and under 7(4) the chaplain must be "clergyman of the Church of England." Section 53(3) requires Welsh prison chaplains to be clergy of the Church in Wales. Only the Anglican Church and Church of England are obligated to have chaplains. Under Prison Rule 14(2) "the chaplain shall visit daily all prisoners belonging to the Church of England who are sick, under restraint or undergoing cellular confinement; and a

---

17 NHS England (December 2013) at 14.1.
18 See the Department of Health website: www.dh.gov.uk (accessed 25 July 2025).
19 network-health.org.uk (accessed 25 July 2025).
20 www.enhcc.eu (accessed 25 July 2025).
21 NHS chaplaincy, Guidelines for NHS managers on pastoral, spiritual and religious care, available at www.england.nhs.uk/wp-content/uploads/2023/08/B1073i-nhs-chaplaincy-guidelines-for-nhs-managers-on-pastoral-spiritual-and-religious-care-august-23.pdf (accessed 25 July 2025)

prison minister shall do the same, as far as he reasonably can, for prisoners of his denomination."[22]

The Prison Act 1952 and the Prison Rules 1999 mandate that prisoners should have the legal right to chaplaincy services. Every prison must have a chaplain and, if needed, can also have an assistant chaplain.[23] However, each must be clergy of the Church of England (or, for prisons in Wales, of the Church in Wales).[24] Chaplains are appointed by the Secretary of State but may only officiate under a licence from the bishop.[25] The government is responsible for paying the chaplains.

The Secretary of State may also appoint a "prison minister" of another denomination, but no prisoner may be visited against his will by such a minister.[26] Typically, a Roman Catholic priest and a Methodist minister are appointed to every prison and other ministers are appointed or called when necessary. The Prison Service Chaplaincy, based at Prison Service Headquarters, is the organisation responsible for religious activity in Prison Service institutions.[27]

Upon arrival to prison, the governor is obliged to document the religious denomination to which the prisoner belongs.[28] This ensures that Article 9 rights are being followed.[29] The minister of that denomination receives a list of the prisoners and only has the permission to visit these prisoners.[30] Prisoners that do not belong to the Church of England must be allowed to attend chapel or to be visited by the Church of England chaplain. Should a prisoner want it, a chaplain must visit any prisoner not of the Church of England in three instances: when a prisoner is sick, under restraint or undergoing cellular confinement, or is not regularly visited by a minister of his own denomination.[31]

The governor must do what they reasonably can to arrange regular visits by a minister in the event that a prisoner has a religion outside of the chaplains available.[32]

The chaplain or prison minister must also interview every prisoner of his denomination individually soon after the prisoner's reception into that prison and

---

22 Emphasis added: for a detailed discussion see Rivers, (note 3), p. 215–220.
23 Prison Act 1952, s. 7.
24 Prison Act 1952, s. 53.
25 Prison Act 1952, ss. 7, 9.
26 Prison Act 1952, s. 10. For an unsuccessful attempt to challenge pay disparity between Church of England and other chaplains see Naeem v. Secretary of State for Justice [2015] EWCA Civ 1264 which was affirmed, albeit on different grounds, by the Supreme Court in Essop and Others v Home Office (UK Border Agency) and Naeem v Secretary of State for Justice [2017] UKSC 27.
27 Prison Service Standing Order 7A.
28 Prison Act 1952, s. 10(5).
29 X v United Kingdom (1983) 5 EHRR 487.
30 Prison Act 1952, s. 10(5).
31 Prison Rules 1999, reg. 14.
32 Ibid., reg. 15.

before his release.[33] Such chaplain must also conduct divine service for prisoners belonging to the Church of England at least once every Sunday, Christmas Day and Good Friday, and celebrations of Holy Communion and weekday services.[34]

Prisoners must not be required to do any unnecessary work on Sunday, Christmas Day or Good Friday if they are Christian. Prisoners of other religions similarly must not be required to do any such work on their recognised days of religious observance.[35] There must be available for the personal use of every prisoner such religious books recognised by his denomination as long as they are approved by the Secretary of State.[36]

Prisoners may request a diet that caters to their religious beliefs.[37] Prisoners are still expected to wear clothing provided by the prison.[38] Nonetheless, they must be allowed to wear religious dress which accords with the requirements of their religion.[39]

In Scotland, Section 3(2) of the Prisons Act 1989 requires each prison to have as chaplain "a minister or a licentiate of the Church of Scotland" to be appointed by the Secretary of State for Scotland. Section 9 makes a provision for the appointment of prison ministers[40] of other religions where "the number of prisoners who belong to a religious denomination other than the Church of Scotland [...]" appears to the Scottish Government's Justice Secretary to require it. The Secretary of State "may pay a minister [so] appointed [...] such remuneration as he thinks reasonable." Importantly, "No prisoner shall be visited against his will by such a minister [...] but every prisoner not belonging to the Church of Scotland shall be allowed, in accordance with the arrangements in force in the prison in which he is confined, to attend chapel or to be visited by the chaplain."[41] Traditionally, the overall service is followed under an agreement between the Scottish Prison Service, the Church of Scotland and the Roman Catholic Church.[42]

In certain parts of the UK, Rules 13 to 19 of the Prison Rules 1999 (as amended), Part 6 of the Prisons and Young Offenders Institutions (Scotland) Rules 2011 and Part VI of the Prison and Young Offenders Centres Rules (Northern Ireland) 1995 all give the right to chaplaincy services.

---

33 Ibid., reg. 14.
34 Prison Rules 1999, reg. 16.
35 Ibid., reg. 18.
36 Ibid., reg. 19.
37 Prison Service Order 4550: Religion Manual.
38 Prison Rules 1999, reg. 23.
39 Prison Service Order 4550: Religion Manual.
40 Non-Anglican prison chaplains in England and Wales were until recently described as "prison ministers" rather than as chaplains; in Scotland the distinction in title is still maintained.
41 Prisons (Scotland) Act 1989, s. 9.
42 See *Brown/Green/Mair*, Religion in Scots Law, Report of an Audit at the University of Glasgow, 2016, Edinburgh, p. 241–242.

While the European Convention does not require that *all* prisoners should have the right to vote, England has reconsidered its old voting laws.[43] As of 2023, a new law permits prisoners to vote who are "held on remand awaiting trial/sentencing; civil prisoners–normally those in prison for failure to pay fines or debts or contempt; offenders on home detention curfew or released on temporary licence."[44]

III.4 Asylum seekers

Asylum seekers have two options, either to live in the community under strict reporting conditions or instead be held in Immigration Removal Centres (IRCs). The Church of England's lead bishop on chaplaincy in IRC's has observed that such spaces are places of prayer.[45] Most centres have a chapel, mosque and multi-faith prayer room. One of the grounds on which those claiming asylum based on a well-founded fear of persecution in their home country, is because of their religious belief. The Immigration and Asylum Tribunal often assesses the genuineness of a religious conversion, and chaplains can be invited by the Tribunal to give evidence on such claims.

III.5 Universities

In modern-day universities, chaplains will most likely be provided by the churches themselves: either full-time or half-time chaplains from the Roman Catholic Church, the Church of England and the major Free Churches supplemented by unpaid chaplains from smaller denominations.[46] Historic arrangements may govern the chaplaincy of a particular denominations. The cost of maintaining a chaplain might be paid by the university but housed may be provided by the corresponding denomination. A report commissioned by the Church of England, *Faiths in Higher*

---

43 See, most recently, McHugh & others v United Kingdom (Application no. 51987/08 and 1,014 others), 10 February 2015.

44 *Johnston*, Prisoners' voting rights, House of Commons Library. researchbriefings.files.parliament.uk/documents/CBP-7461/CBP-7461.pdf

45 *Rt Revd Colin Fletcher*, Bishop of Dorchester, Church Times, 28 March 2012.

46 See Aune/Guest/Law, Chaplains on Campus: Understanding Chaplaincy in UK Universities (2019): www.churchofengland.org/sites/default/files/2019-05/chaplains_on_campus_full_report_final_pdf_.pdf (accessed 25 July 2025).

Education Chaplaincy, found that much chaplaincy work in tertiary education was voluntary and that the volunteers came disproportionately from minority faiths.[47]

III.6 Schools

In Voluntary Aided and Voluntary Controlled schools, the schools themselves are of a religious character chaplaincy and thus will be supplied by the parent denomination but not always by a designated chaplain.[48]

In Scotland, there are no statutory obligations on such schools to appoint chaplains, nor to favour the ministry of the Church of Scotland; and "it appears from anecdotal evidence that at least some non-denominational schools do not appoint chaplains at all."[49]

III.7 Parliament, courts, police and industry

Chaplains who operate in courts and tribunals minister to litigants, witnesses, jurors, lawyers, staff and judges. Their attendance at court is on a part-time basis and is not financed by the Court Service. Their renumeration comes from spaces like Workplace Ministry or, of an independent charity set up to supply chaplains to the local courts. Typically, these chaplains are predominantly from Christian denominations, although there exists a part-time Muslim chaplain in Bradford.

When it comes to gray spaces such as the workforce, the Oil Chaplaincy was formed in the 1980s; it provides services to the oil and gas industry through off-shore visits, a counselling service, material support, and special services in a chapel in the Kirk of St Nicholas, Aberdeen.[50] The Association of Civil Aviation Chaplaincies typically funds prayer rooms in UK airports.[51] At sea, the charity Missions to Seafarers, provides spiritual and practical assistances to workers on ships who are away from their homes and families for long periods of time. Lastly, the National Association of Chaplains to the Police provides chaplaincy to the police force.[52]

---

47 Almost one-third are from the Baha'i, Buddhist, Hindu, Jewish, Muslim and Sikh faith-communities.

48 *Church of England Archbishops' Council Education Division*, The Public Face of God: Chaplaincy in Anglican Secondary Schools and Academies in England and Wales, April 2014.

49 Ibid., 4.7.2.

50 *Rivers*, (note 3), p. 225.

51 *Rivers*, (note 3), p. 226.

52 *Armitage*, Police Chaplaincy – Servant to the Service, September 1996, Home Office.

III.8 Islam and other religions

According to the 2021 Census, 3.9 million respondents in England and Wales identified as Muslim.[53] In 2007, Dr Ataullah Siddiqui of the Markfield Institute of Higher Education discovered that "Chaplaincy for Muslims has in general been both tentative and precarious. Muslims as a whole are only just catching on to the idea of chaplaincy."[54]

IV. Employment status of chaplains

Most ministers are treated as employees with regard to employment rights: for example, full-time prison chaplains are employed by the relevant prisons service, NHS chaplains by NHS trusts and military chaplains under the King's Commission.

V. Conclusion

The freedom of belief found within Article 9 of the European Convention on Human Rights became enforceable in the United Kingdom by virtue of the Human Rights Act 1998. Yet, while freedom of religion is integral, the support for chaplaincy has garnered criticism because of its religious nature. The National Secular Society reported that in 2020/21, the NHS spent £ 29 m. Considering inflation, it appears that chaplaincy funding has general decreased.

---

53 See www.ons.gov.uk/peoplepopulationandcommunity/culturalidentity/religion/articles/religionbyageandsexenglandandwales/census2021 (accessed 25 July 2025).

54 The Institute, established in 2000 in association with Loughborough University, holds short courses in chaplaincy: see www.mihe.ac.uk/muslim-chaplaincy (accessed 25 July 2025).

Spiritual Care in Public Institutions in the Federal Republic of Germany and its Federal States (Länder)

Provisions in Constitutions and Treaties between State and Church and Practical Realization[1]

FELIX HAMMER

I. Spiritual care in public institutions in Germany – overview

I.1 Intensive legal regulations in Germany

For spiritual care in public institutions[2] exists in Germany – so as for other sectors of public life – a very voluminous legislation and regulation with directions in the constitutions of the Federal Republic of Germany and their member states, in laws, in treaties between the state and churches and religious communities and at last in administrative agreements frequent between ministries and religious communities. Partly the Federal Republic has the competence for the regulation (namely for spiritual care in the armed forces[3] – art. 73 sec. 1 no. 1 Basic Law – and for officers in the police forces of the Federal Republic[4] – art. 73 sec. 1 no. 8

---

1 Abbreviations: BVerfG = Bundesverfassungsgericht / German Federal Constitutional Court; ed. = editor; HSKR³ = *Pirson/Rüfner/Germann/Muckel* (ed.), Handbuch des Staatskirchenrechts der Bundesrep. Deutschland, 3rd ed. 3 vol., 2020, Berlin; KirchE = Entscheidungen in Kirchensachen / Collection of Decisions of German Courts in ecclesiastical and religious litigations.

2 Overviews: *Tretera/Horák* (ed.), Spiritual Care in Public Institutions in Europe, 2019, Berlin, and there: *Robbers*, The Legal Status of Pastoral Care in Public Institutions in Germany, p. 12–20; *Schilberg*, Krankenhausseelsorge, Seelsorge im Strafvollzug und anderen Anstalten, in: HSKR³, vol. 2, p. 2343–2371; *Ennuschat/Hauschildt*, Anstaltsseelsorge, in: *Heun* et. al. (ed.), Evang. Staatslexikon, new ed. 2006, Sp.62–67.

3 *Ennuschat*, Militärseelsorge in Deutschland: Verfassungsrechtl. u. rechtspolit. Perspektiven, ZevKR, 64 (2019), 107–124; *Ennuschat*, Seelsorge in der Bundeswehr, in: HSKR³, vol. 2, p. 2295–2327; *Heimann*, Zukunftsperspektiven der Militärseelsorge, ZevKR, 64 (2019), p. 125–142; *Hierold*, Militärseelsorge im Spannungsfeld zwischen Kirche und Staat, AfkKR 175 (2006), p. 100–112; *Kruk*, Die Militärseelsorge, KuR 2001, p. 67–86; *Mehrle*, Trennung vom Staat – Mitarbeit in staatl. Institutionen, 1999, Berlin.

4 Vereinbarung über d. evang. Seelsorge im Bundesgrenzschutz v. 12.08.1965, Bek. des Bundesinnenministers v. 18.10.1965 (Gem. MinBl. p. 374, i. d. F. d. Änderung v. 01.07.1968/08.05.1969); Vereinb. über

Basic Law), partly its member states (for all sectors which are simply a part of culture – and religion mostly and spiritual care always are a part of culture). After all – the large number of provisions in constitutions, laws, treaties and administrative agreements secures the rights of religious communities to spiritual care, gives spiritual care in public institutions a firm contour and all, who are involved here, legal certainty.

I.2 Appearances of spiritual care in public institutions

The constitution of the German Reich from the year 1919, the constitution of Weimar, which first guaranteed spiritual care in public institutions[5] named only as institutions in question the ground forces of the army, hospitals, prisons and other public institutions, in which men were not allowed to just leave the institution, whenever they wanted to get spiritual help or were in urgent need of it. The Basic Law of the Federal Republic of Germany[6] and some of the early constitutions of its member states[7] repeated this wording. However since then a lot of further similar forms of spiritual care arose, for example spiritual care in the police forces[8] and for fire fighters,[9] in railway stations[10] and airports,[11] in universities[12] and even

---

d. kath. Seelsorge im Bundesgrenzschutz v. 12.08.1965, Bek. d. BMI v. 18.10.1965 (Gem. MinBl. p. 377).

5 Art. 141 Verfassung des Deutschen Reichs v. 11.08.1919 (RGBl. p. 1383) – WRV.

6 Art. 140 Basic Law/art. 141 WRV (note 5).

7 Art. 148 constitution Bayern v. 02.12.1946; art. 62 Bremen v. 21.10.1947; art. 54 Hessen v. 01.12.1946; art. 20 Nordrhein-Westfalen v.28.06.1950; art. 48 Rheinland-Pfalz v. 18.05.1947; art. 42 Saarland v. 15.12.1947.

8 *Heintzen*, Polizeiseelsorge, in: HSKR[3], vol. 2, p. 2329–2341; *Blanke/Jaschke/Manzke/v. Sachsen Brand* (ed.), 50 Jahre Seelsorgevereinbarung in Bundesgrenzschutz und Bundespolizei, 2015, Göttingen.

9 Konzeption für die Feuerwehrseelsorge der Erzdiöz. Freiburg u. d. Diöz. Rottenburg-Stuttgart in Bad.-Württ. v. 04.05.2022 (KABl. Rottenb.-Stuttg. p. 220); *Deißenböck*, Umgang mit Sterben und Tod im Feuerwehrdienst – eine Chance für die Seelsorge?!, 2019, Würzburg.

10 *Nikles*, Bahnhofsmission u. Bahnhofsdienste in Deutschland. Ein historischer Abriss ihrer Aufgaben- u. Organisationsentwickl., 2019, Opladen/Berlin/Toronto; *Nikles*, Soziale Hilfe am Bahnhof. Zur Geschichte d. Bahnhofsmission in Deutschland (1894–1960), Freiburg/Br. 1994; www.bahnhofsmission.de/index.php?id=3 (accessed 25 July 2025).

11 Maader, Flughafenseelsorge, in: Stimmen der Zeit, vol. 217 (1999)/5, p. 353–354; Maader, Seelsorge und Jets. Ökumen. Flughafenseelsorge, in: Diakonia, 5 (1974)/1, p. 59–61; *Meier/Cimaschi-Oberti*, Seelsorge im Katastrophenfall. Erfahrungen aus der Flughafenseelsorge, in: Diakonia, 30 (1999)/5, p. 346–350; www.airportchapel.de/ (accessed 25 July 2025).

12 *Hirschberg/Freudenberg/Plisch* (ed.), Handbuch Studierendenseelsorge, 2022, Göttingen; *Hierold*, Schul- und Hochschulseelsorge, in: *Haering/Rees/Schmitz* (ed.), Handbuch des Kath. Kirchenrechts, 3rd ed. 2015, p. 776–777; *Bischof* (ed.), Kath. Hochschulseelsorge zwischen Akzeptanz und Ablehnung. Zur Geschichte d. Kath. Hochschulseelsorge an d. Univ. München 1927 bis 2007, 2008, Haar/München.

in public schools[13] and above all an emergency pastoral care for great disasters in the public sphere (railway, airplane and traffic accidents and mass shootings).[14] They surely were developed gradually on the basis of spiritual care in public institutions. Common is all these forms of spiritual care, that people, who use a public institution, who are working for it or who are affected by an accident or disaster in the public sphere, need in special situations urgently spiritual help and can't get it in the usual way by contacting a pastor. Typical is, that a risk, which is connected with some public institutions has come to fruition: The traumatization of police officers and fire fighters by terrible disasters and criminal acts, disorientation at railway stations, fear of flying in the airports, the loneliness of the single student in the university, to be a failure at public school and nobody will help. According to this development current treaties with religious communities don't use the term "spiritual care in public institutions" but instead "special fields of spiritual care",[15] "spiritual care in special institutions",[16] "spiritual care in special cases"[17] or "special spiritual care".[18] And occasionally in this context the emergency pastoral care by the state is guaranteed explicitly,[19] but in most cases no special legal guarantee exists for these forms of spiritual care with the exception of spiritual care for police forces.[20] But meanwhile these forms of spiritual care are regulated detailed in a lot of administrative agreements with churches and religious communities[21] just as

---

13 *Jacobs*, Evang. Schulseelsorge. Grundlagen, Vertraulichkeit, Strukturprobleme, KuR, 25 (2019) p. 9–20; *Meckel/Haydn-Quindeau*, Schulseelsorge, in: *Hallermann* et al. (ed.), Lexikon für Kirchen- und Religionsrecht, vol. 4, 2021; *Gutmann/Kuhlmann/Meuche* (ed.), Praxisbuch Schulseelsorge, 2014, Göttingen.

14 *Ahlers*, Notfallseelsorge als eine Form der Sonderseelsorge und ihre kirchenrechtl. Implikationen, in: *Althaus* et al. (ed.), Festschrift f. Reinhardt, 2007, p. 21–30; *Brandt/Grommek* (ed.), Opferbetreuung und Notfallseelsorge, 2018, Rothenburg/Oberlausitz.

15 Vertr. d. Landes Berlin mit d. Evang. Kirche Berlin-Brandenburg-schlesische Oberlausitz v. 20.02.2006 (GVBl. Berlin p. 715), art. 15.

16 Vertr. zw. d. Land Schlesw.-Holst. u. d. Heiligen Stuhl v.12.01.2009 (Schl.-Holst. GVOBl. 2009, 264), art. 8; Vertrag zw. d. Land Brandenburg u. d. Jüdischen Gemeinde v. 11.01.2005 (GVBl. I p. 158), art. 3; Vertr. zw. d. Freien Hansestadt Bremen u. d. Islamischen Religionsgemeinschaften im Lande Bremen v. 15.01.2013 (Drs. 18/727 v. 15.01.2013), art. 7.

17 Vertrag d. Landes Baden-Württemberg mit der Evang. Landeskirche in Baden und m. d. Evang. Landeskirche in Württ. v. 17.10.2007 (GBl. Bad.-Württ. 2008, p. 2), art. 16.

18 Vertr. zw. d. Heiligen Stuhl u. d. Freistaat Sachsen v. 02.07.1996 (SächsGVBl. 1997 p. 18), art. 12.

19 Evang. Kirchenvertr. Bad. Württ. (note 17), art. 16 sec. 3.

20 For example: Verfassung d. Landes Brandenburg v. 20.08.1992, art. 38; Vertr. zw. d. Heiligen Stuhl u. d. Land Sachsen-Anhalt v. 15.01.1998 (GVBl. LSA 1998, p. 160), art. 10 sec. 2; Vertr. Berlin u. Evang. Kirche Berlin-Brandenburg-schles. Oberlausitz (note 15), art. 15; Vertr. zw. d. Freien u. Hansestadt Hamburg u. d. Jüdischen Gemeinde in Hamburg v. 20.06.2007 (HmbGVBl. 2007, 407), art. 5; Vertr. zw. Bremen u. d. Islamischen Religionsgem. (note 16), art. 7 sec. 1.

21 For example: Vereinbarung über d. evang. Seelsorge im Bundesgrenzschutz v. 12.08.1965; Vereinb. über d. evang. Seelsorge in d. hessischen Vollzugspolizei v. 30.05.1984; Vereinb. zw. d. Land Sachsen-Anhalt u. d. Evang. Landeskirchen in Sachsen-Anhalt über d. kirchl. Dienst an Polizeibeamten (Polizeiseelsorgevereinb.) v. 30.06.1994 (ABl. Landeskirche Anhalt 1995 p. 3); Vereinb. über d. Zusam-

in ecclesiastical rules and instructions[22] – and they are customary everywhere in Germany. So spiritual care in public institutions over the past decades became part of a wide range of different forms of specialized spiritual care – they all try to help people in situations of spiritual distress.

II. The constitutional and legal foundation of spiritual care in public institutions

II.1 Constitutional provisions

Provisions, which guarantee spiritual care in public institutions are to be found not only in the "Grundgesetz" – Basic Law/constitution – of the Federal Republic of Germany, but also in most of the constitutions of the member states of the Federal Republic.[23] The Grundgesetz has no wording of its own, but took over the art. 141 of the former constitution of the German Reich of 1919 and incorporated its text into the new constitution without any modifications. The constitutions of the member states, some of them created before the Grundgesetz, partly later, all have the same or very similar regulations, either by incorporation of art. 140 Basic Law or art. 141 constitution of the German Reich, or by repeating the text of art. 141 of 1919 similarly. Important is the fact, that all of the constitutional provisions in Germany order explicitly, that participation in religious services and spiritual care must be voluntarily and there must not be any pressure. Nevertheless the spiritual care in public institutions is in the German constitutional law very firmly established, first and foremost because the constitutional law of the member states must follow the fundamental principles, which the Grundgesetz of the Federal Republic defines for Germany.

---

menarbeit in d. Notfallseelsorge zw. d. Land Baden-Württ. u. d. Evang. Landeskirche in Baden, der Evang. Landeskirche in Württ., der Diöz. Rottenburg-Stuttgart u. d Erzdiöz. Freiburg (KABl. Rottenb.-Stuttg., 113 [2006], p. 305–306); *Blanke/Jaschke/Manzke/v. Sachsen Brand* (note 8), 2015.

22 For example: Ordnung f. d. Notfallseelsorge in d. Diöz. Augsburg (ABl. Diöz. Augsburg, 123 [2013], p. 321); Ordnung d. Notfallseelsorge in Berlin v. 11.09.2002 (ABl. Bischöfl. Ord. Berlin, 74 [2002], p. 92); Rahmenordnung f. d. Notfallseelsorge im Bistum Mainz v. 07.11.2003 (KABl. Diöz. Mainz, 146 [2004], p. 7); Rahmenordnung f. d. Notfallseelsorge im Bistum Trier v. 12.12.2007 (KABl. Bistum Trier, 152 [2008], p. 24–25).

23 12 of 16 states: Art. 5/art. 140 GG/art. 141 WRV Bad.-Württ.; art. 148 Bayern; art. 138 Brandenburg; art. 62 Bremen; art. 54 Hessen; art. 9/art. 141 WRV Mecklenb.-Vorp.; art. 20 Nordrh.-Westf.; art. 48 Rheinl.-Pf.; art. 42 Saarland; art. 109 sec. 4/141 WRV Sachsen; art. 32 sec. 5/141 WRV Sachsen-Anh.; art. 40/140 GG/141 WRV Thüringen.

II.2 Provisions in treaties between the State and the churches and religious communities

The warranties of the constitutions for spiritual care in public institutions will be complemented by treaties between churches and religious communities and the member states of the Federal Republic,[24] which are in charge of the legislation and regulation on the sector of culture – and religion and spiritual care are as already stated, part of culture. Treaties, which are settling questions of spiritual care are existing not only between the Catholic[25] and the Protestant[26] Churches and the member states, but also with non-Christian communities, especially with Jewish religious communities,[27] the community of the Alevis in Germany[28] and currently – but only a few treaties – with Muslim or Islamic religious communities or associations.[29] The provisions here are formulated more extensive and comprehensive or with more details as the guarantees of the constitutions. The regulations in the treaties incorporate the rules of the constitution, secure the protection frame and take into account the special details of the different spiritual beliefs and needs. If

---

24 *Isensee*, Anstaltsseelsorge und Diakonie in den Kirchenvertr. d. Freist. Sachsen, in: *Uhle* (ed.), 20 Jahre Staatskirchenverträge in Sachsen, 2016, p. 87–107; *Rink*, Diener zweier Herren?, ZevKR, 64 (2019), 183–187.

25 So bereits art. 11 Konk. zw. Seiner Heiligkeit Papst Pius XI. u. d. Staate Bayern v. 29.03.1924 (GVBl. 1925, p. 530); art. 11 Konk. zw. d. Hl. Stuhle u. d. Land Niedersachsen v. 26.02.1965 (A. A. S., vol. LVII [1965], Nr. 12, p. 834–856); art. 12 & Schlußprot. Vertr. zw. d. Hl. Stuhl u. d. Freistaat Sachsen v. 02.07.1996 (SächsGVBl. 1997 p. 18), and others.

26 Art. 17 Vertr. zw. d. Bayer. Staate u. d. Evang.-Luth. Kirche in Bayern rechts des Rheins v. 15.11.1924 (GVBl. 1925, p. 53); art. 6 Vertr. d. Evang. Landeskirchen in Nieders. m. d. Lande Niedersachsen (Loccumer Vertrag) v. 19.03.1955 (Nds. GVBl. Sb. I p. 369); art. 16 Evang. Kirchenvertr. Bad. Württ. (note 17) and others more.

27 So: Vertr. zw. d. Bundesrep. Deutschland u. d. Zentralrat d. Juden in Dtschld. z. Regelung d. jüd. Militärseelsorge v. 20.12.2019 (BGBl. 2020 I p. 1665); Vertr. d. Landes Bad.-Württ. mit d. Israelit. Religionsgemeinschaft Baden u. d. Israelit. Rel.gem. Württembergs v. 18.01.2010 (GBl. p. 302), art. 3 & Schlussprot.: Jüd. Religion u. Seelsorge; Staatsvertr. über d. Beziehungen d. Landes Berlin z. Jüd. Gemeinde Berlin v. 19.11.1993, Vertragsges. v. 08.02.1994 (GVBl. p. 67), art. 3: Seelsorger. Betreuung der Mitglieder d. Jüd. Gemeinde zu Berlin in öffentl. u. nichtöffentl. Einrichtungen; Vertr. zw. d. Land Brandenburg u. d. Jüd. Gemeinde v. 11.01.2005, Vertragsges. v. 26.04.2005 (GVBl. I p. 158), art. 3: Seelsorge in besonderen Einrichtungen; Vert. zw. d. Freien u. Hansestadt Hamburg u. d. Jüd. Gemeinde in Hamburg, v. 20.06.2007, Vertragsges. v.27.11.2007 (HmbGVBl. p. 407), art. 5 & Protokollerkl.: Seelsorge.

28 Vertr. zw. d. Freien u. Hansest. Hamburg u. d. Alevitischen Gemeinde Deutschland e. V. v. 13.11.2012 (Drucks. 20/5830), Zust. durch die Hamb. Bürgerschaft 13.06.2013, art. 7 & Protokollerkl.: Religiöse Betreuung in besonderen Einrichtungen; Vertr. zw. d. Land Rheinland-Pfalz u. d. Alevitischen Gemeinde Deutschland e. V. v. 09.04.2019, art. 7: Religiöse Betreuung in besonderen Einrichtungen.

29 Vertr. zw. d. Freien u. Hansest. Hamburg, d. DITIB-Landesverband Hamburg, SCHURA – Rat der Islamischen Gemeinschaften in Hamburg u. d. Verband d. Islam. Kulturzentren v. 13.11.2012 (Drs. 20/5830 v. 13.11.2012), art. 7: Relig. Betreuung in besonderen Einrichtungen; Vertr. zw. d. Freien Hansest. Bremen u. d. Islam. Religionsgemeinschaften im Lande Bremen, v. 15.01.2013 (Drs. 18/727 v. 15.01.2013), art. 7: Relig. Betreuung in besonderen Einrichtungen.

there might be a constitutional amendment to the disadvantage of churches and religious communities, there would still be the regulations in the treaties. The state would have to ignore or break these regulations if it wanted to stop or hinder spiritual care in public institutions. And this would be absolutely unthinkable in a modern constitutional state. The treaties for spiritual care in the armed forces are between the churches and religious communities and the Federal Republic, which is the legislative organ to regulate the matters of defence (art. 73 sec. 1 no. 1 GG), as partners,[30] so as the agreements for the police of the Federal Republic.[31]

II.3 Provisions in the laws of the Federal Republic and their member states (Länder) and in administrative agreements

The guarantees of spiritual care in public institutions in the constitutions of the Federal Republic of Germany and their member states and in the treaties between the state and the churches or religious communities take shape partly in different laws partly in administrative agreements between state and religious communities. In these specified regulations various details concerning the organization and the carrying out of the spiritual care are regulated, for example the conditions of safety in prisons,[32] the voluntariness of the use of spiritual care,[33] the protection of patients, who want no spiritual care, and of their data in hospitals.[34] Especially in sectors, where the fundamental rights of citizens and of the religious communities are not touched or seriously affected, it is not necessary to have legal regulation.[35] There or where the guidelines of the laws only are to be specified[36] the details of

---

30 Vertr. zw. d. Evang. Kirche in Dtschld. u. d. Bundesrep. Deutschland z. Regelung d. evang. Militärseelsorge v. 22.02.1957 (BGBl. II p. 702); Vert. zw. d. Bundesrep. Deutschland u. d. Zentralrat der Juden in Deutschland z. Regelung d. jüd. Militärseels. v. 20.12.2019 (BGBl. 2020 I p. 1665); *Rink*, ZevKR, 64 (2019), p. 183–187.

31 Cf. note 4: Vereinbarungen über d. evang. u. kath. Seelsorge im Bundesgrenzschutz.

32 §§ 29 sec. 2, 30 sec. 3 Drittes Buch Justizvollzugsgesetzbuch – Strafvollzug Bad.-Württ. (art. 1 Ges. v. 10.11.2009, GBl. p. 545).

33 § 36 Ges. über d. Rechtsstellung der Soldaten i. d. F. d. Bek. v. 30.05.2005 (BGBl. I p. 1482).

34 Landeskrankenhausges. Bad.-Württ. (LKHG) i. d. F. v. 29.11.2007, § 45 sec. 2; *K. W. Schwarz*, Wieviel Seelsorge verträgt das Krankenhaus?, öarr 62 (2015), 38–48.

35 Vereinb. über d. Wahrnehmung d. evang. Polizeiseelsorge im Lande Schlesw.-Holst. v. 30.08.1978; Vereinb. über d. evang. Seelsorge in d. hessischen Vollzugspolizei v. 30.05.1984; Vereinb. zw. d. Land Sachsen-Anh. u. d. Evang. Landeskirchen in Sachs.-Anh. über d. kirchl. Dienst an Polizeibeamten (Polizeiseelsorgevereinb.) v. 30.06.1994 (ABl. Landesk. Anhalt 1995 p. 3).

36 Vereinb. d. Freistaats Sachsen mit d. Evang. Kirchen im Freist. Sachsen z. Regelung d. seelsorgerischen Tätigkeit in d. Justizvollzugsanstalten v. 25.01.1993; Vereinb. zw. d. Land Brandenburg u. d. Evang. Kirche in Berlin-Brandenb. über d. Seelsorge in Justizvollzugsanst. v. 02.11./02.12.1993; Vereinb. zw. d. Land Sachsen-Anh. u. d. Evang. Kirchen im Land Sachsen-Anh. z. Regelung d. seelsorg. Tätigkeit in d. Justizvollzugsanst. v 24.03.1994; Vereinb. über d. Wahrnehmung d. evang. Seelsorge in d. Justizvollzugseinrichtungen in Schlesw.-Holst. v. 01.11.2019.

spiritual care can and will be regulated by administrative agreements between the legally responsible ministries or other departments and the Catholic and Protestant Church (repeatedly with both together)[37] or the other religious communities. All these regulations together provide a framework for spiritual care in public institutions in Germany, that allows working and caring in safe and legally secure circumstances.

III. From spiritual care in public institutions to spiritual care in cases of extreme situations in the public sphere

III.1 From spiritual care in public institutions to spiritual care in public installations or services and in the case of public disasters

As described spiritual care in public institutions has developed during the last decades, expanded and changed, because in a progressive, modern society the needs of the people regarding spiritual care are more and more complex, specific spiritual care is crucial.

So the subject got wider and more relevant. However spiritual care in public institutions is an important task for the churches, then similar forms of spiritual care developed, for example spiritual care for police forces, at universities, on airports or emergency pastoral care. So these days spiritual care in public institutions changed into or was supplemented by spiritual care in public entities and services and in cases of public disasters.

III.2 Spiritual care in public services and special public cases not protected by art. 140 GG/141 WRV, but by art. 4 sec. 1 and 2 GG

Spiritual care in public services or in special public cases is not protected by art. 140 GG/141 WRV, because this norm demands clearly an institution, in which people must stay and cannot get spiritual help in the usual ways. But this form of spiritual care is protected by the general guarantee of freedom of faith and religion (art. 4 sec. 1 and 2 GG). The Federal Constitutional Court says that practice of religion implies also all prayers, religious teaching and education, observing of re-

37 Vereinbarung Notfallseelsorge (note 21); Vereinb. zw. d. Innenministerium Bad.-Württ. u. d. Evang. Oberkirchenrat Karlsruhe, d. Evang. Oberkirchenrat Stuttgart, d. Erzbischöfl. Ord. Freiburg u. d. Bischöfl. Ord. Rottenburg über d. Kirchl. Arbeit in d. Polizei d. Landes Bad.-Württ., Bekanntmachg. d. Oberkirchenrats Stuttgart v. 13.12.2017 (Abl. 67 p. 351); Vereinb. über d. Polizeiseelsorge der ev. und kath. Kirchen mit d. Land Rheinl.-Pf. v. 13.08.1974 u. 14.02.1975.

ligious traditions etc.,[38] so that all forms of spiritual care are subject of the freedom of worship and protected by art. 4 GG. But considering the case law of the Constitutional Court the protection of the general freedom of faith and religion may be as extensive as the special protection for spiritual care in public institutions.

IV. Spiritual care in public institutions of a secular state

IV.1 The Federal Republic of Germany: a secular, but not a laicistic state

The Grundgesetz and the constitutions of the German states define themselves as secular states, which means there is no state church or no particularly privileged faith. But there does not have to be a strong separation between church and state. The state may not identify with a religion, it may not have a special idea of God and religious truth, but it may help its citizens and their churches and religious communities to believe and to be religious as they see it to be right and proper. Only the state itself is not allowed to identify with a special religion and to do missionary work for special religions or for religion or faith at all and it also can't interfere in matters of atheism. It can work with religious communities in freedom, it provides for the freedom of worship, it takes care that everyone has a right to the dignity of human life and to the free development of his personality.[39] And so it may offer spiritual care in the public institutions of the state, but it may not try to take sides for using it – it must be completely neutral. Therefore, many of the constitutional and legal provisions for spiritual care emphasize, that there is no pressure to accept spiritual care.[40] And the state cannot decide, in which way spiritual care has to take place – that's strictly the affair of the religious communities, which have the fundamental freedom of faith and religion.

IV.2 Welfare state and care for wellbeing of the citizens

The modern welfare state not only grants its citizens freedom and security, and the right to look out for his or her own self and fortune, today it helps its people in many and diverse ways to realise their fundamental rights (for example: the free-

---

38 BVerfGE 24, 236 – Aktion Rumpelkammer; BVerfG KirchE 48, 398 = DVBl 2007, 119 = DÖV 2007, 202 – Mun.

39 BVerfGE 19, 206; BVerfGE 137, 273 = KirchE 64, 305 = JZ 2015, 188 m. Anm. *Classen* & *Rixen* – head doctor in Düsseldorf; BVerfGE 153, 1= NVwZ 2020, 461 m. Anm. *v. Schwanenflug* = JZ 2020, 405 m. Anm. *Classen* – headscarf.

40 Art. 141 WRV (note 5); art. 148 constitution Bayern; art. 62 const. Bremen; art. 54 const. Hessen; art. 20 const. Nordrh.-Westf.; § 36 Soldatengesetz Federal Republic.

dom to choose a career by offering different schools and universities), it can also support people, who need urgent spiritual help in difficult or life-threatening situations. Because of this it can provide for institutions, which can offer spiritual care. As a secular state it is not able to serve in this field itself (because the state does not know about God and religion), and it does not identify with special religions or religion in general or favour or promote one or some of them.[41] But if the state respects all this, it may not only, but it has – in the interest of the freedom of faith and religion of its citizens – to ensure, that they can get spiritual help and care in public institutions, if they are in need – so the secular state supports its citizens in many situations to realise their fundamental rights.

IV.3 Spiritual care and freedom of faith and religion

Spiritual care in public institutions is protected by the freedom of faith, religion and philosophy of life (art. 4 sec. 1 and 2 GG). The constitutional guarantee of spiritual care is a specialized sector of this freedom, but all, what is typical or characteristic for the freedom of religion and worship is also valid for spiritual care in public institutions: The secular state has no idea of the religious truth and can't say, what is religiously right or wrong. Regarding the sermonizing, the prayers or the liturgical or religious behaviour of the pastors in public institutions crucial is the faith and the self-image of the religious community,[42] however the pastors have to respect the constitution and the laws,[43] especially those, which regulate the safety and working order of the public institution. If there is a conflict between freedom of religion and work order of the institution, there has to be an evaluation of both positions – both positions are to be observed and evaluated correctly as best as possible.[44]

IV.4 Spiritual care and guarantee of human dignity (art. 1 sec. 1 GG)

The German Federal Constitutional Court decided in a case of spiritual care in a prison and the pastor's obligation to secrecy,[45] that the conversation with a pastor and confession are protected not only by the freedom of religion and art. 4 GG,

---

41 BVerfG KirchE 54, 54 = NJW 2009, 3151 – Erziehungsrecht; BVerfG KirchE 53, 290 = BVerfGE 123, 148 – jüdische Kultusgemeinden; BVerfGE 93, 1 = NJW 1995, 2477 – Schulkreuz.

42 BVerfGE 24, 236; BVerfG NJW 2015, 1359 = KirchE 65, 26 = BayVBl. 2015, 445/484 m. Anm. *Wolff* = KuR 2015, 105 Ls. m. Anm. *Wittreck*, 103 f.; BVerfG KirchE 67, 319 = NVwZ 2016, 1804.

43 BVerfG DVBl. 2001, 984 – Sektenbeauftragte.

44 BVerfG KuR, 22 (2016), 260 = JZ 2017, 145 m. Anm. *Hillgruber* – Karfreitag; BVerfG NJW 2017, 381 = NVwZ 2017, 549 – Kopftuch.

45 BVerfG KirchE 49, 65 = NJW 2007, 1865.

but they are also protected by the guarantee of human dignity and of art. 1 sec. 1 GG. Art. 1 can't be altered by amendments to the constitution, because art. 79 sec. 3 GG forbids amendments of the principles of art. 1 and 20 GG – and the protection of human dignity is a principle of art. 1 GG. The idea of the Constitutional Court in this decision concerns not only prisons, but also hospitals, the army and all places and situations, in which people need very urgently the help of a pastor, because they are in danger of death, long-term imprisonment or in similar serious situations. Therefore spiritual care in public institutions in its central sector is protected – without the possibility of alterations – also by the constitution's protection of human dignity.

IV.5 Limitations of spiritual care: security of prisons, functionality of hospitals, protection of freedom of religion and protection of data privacy

The constitution's protection for spiritual care in public institutions is not unlimited. The Federal Constitutional Court takes into consideration also the functionality and the safety of prisons, hospitals and the army and demands a consideration of both aspects,[46] because the state under the rule of law and the constitutional democracy are also protected by the constitution (art. 20 sec. 1 up to 3 GG), and the work order of hospitals is necessary to insure the protection of life and health of all people (art. 2 sec. 2 GG). All aspects of the special situation must be considered to find an appropriate, balanced solution. Furthermore, the freedom of religion of the people, who don't want any form of spiritual care (art. 4 GG), must be respected. Furthermore, today the protection of data privacy has also to be observed (art. 2 sec. 1 with art. 1 sec. 1 GG). All these rights are limiting the freedom of spiritual care and there must be a consideration, what's more important: the right of spiritual care or the competing rights. Therefore, spiritual care is only permissible for people, who declare their consent. This is also true for the use of personal data regarding spiritual care. In prisons, hospitals and in the army, people must declare their consent to the offering of spiritual care of a particular religion when they arrive at the institution. But in hospitals there are often people, who can't declare their consent due to sickness, unconsciousness etc. And if their respective families can't say, what these patients want, a priest may visit the patients at their sickbed and if he/she offers a prayer or a blessing this will rarely be considered a relevant violation of the freedom of religion.

---

46 BVerfG KirchE 49, 65 = NJW 2007, 1865, m. n. 20 ss.

V. Spiritual care: a duty of religious denominations and of secular state

The churches and other religious communities have – according to their religious rules – the duty to provide spiritual care for their believers and members by their pastors. But the state also has the duty to give people, who must live or work in its public institutions, the opportunity to receive spiritual care. The Federal Constitutional Court declares that freedom of faith and religion in the constitution contains also a responsibility of the state to treat all people and all religious communities in the same way, and if the state provides benefits, that must be for all in the same way and so all are entitled to these benefits.[47] And because the state guarantees in the constitutions of the Federal Republic and many of their member states and in treaties with religious communities spiritual care in public institutions, people and the religious communities have a right to and the state has a corresponding duty to grant spiritual care everywhere in the public institutions. But the secular state can only give an open frame for the spiritual care to be given, without any provisions regarding worship, God and religious truth.[48] The churches and religious communities fill that open frame with their beliefs and religious rules. Only they have the necessary knowledge and therefore the right to determine the content of the spiritual care they provide. Both – state and religious communities – have a duty to provide for spiritual care in public institutions, but in a very different way. Only the combination of the functions of state and churches amounts to the spiritual care the people in the public institutions need for their spiritual welfare.

VI. Equality of the denominations in the secular state

VI.1 All beliefs and religions are equal before the law

Because the Federal Republic of Germany is a secular state without any state religion (art. 140 GG with art. 137 sec. 1 constitution of 1919), all religious beliefs are equal before the law and may not be used as grounds for discrimination (art. 3 sec. 3 GG). Therefore, the right to offer spiritual care in public institutions is not limited to the main Christian churches, all religious beliefs are allowed to offer spiritual care, if they want it for their members. In treaties with the member states of the Federal Republic – and in the case of spiritual care in the army – with the

---

47 BVerfGE 123, 148 – Förderung jüdischer Kultusgemeinden.

48 BVerfG JZ 2009, 511 m. Anm. *Gärditz* = KirchE 52, 173 = NJW 2009, 2190 – university lecturers; BVerfG NJW 2009, 1195 = KirchE 52, 337 – the right of courts of the state to decide litigations in churches; BVerfGE 137, 273.

Federal Republic[49] Jewish communities[50] and the community of Alevis in Germany[51] are explicitly guaranteed the right to provide spiritual care in public institutions of the respective member state and in the German armed forces.

VI.2 Religious and ideological communities

The Grundgesetz (art. 140) with the constitution of 1919 (art. 137 sec. 7) states, that ideological communities have the same legal status as religious communities. Both enjoy the same rights. So the ideological communities also have the right to provide spiritual care in public institutions as well as the Christian churches and other religious communities, if they wish to offer such a service to their members. But now there are no ideological communities, that are actually offering spiritual care.

VI.3 Not all religions are able to provide spiritual care in public institutions

Although according to the constitution and the law all religious and ideological communities have the right to provide spiritual care in public institutions, not all of them are able to offer it, because they have no suitable pastors or personnel, who are sufficiently trained and who can represent the community and its faith. But in the interest of the people living and working in the institutions, who need spiritual help, the requirements for becoming a spiritual caregiver/pastor are not strict,[52] they do not necessarily need an university degree in theology. But depending on the institution they must meet security requirements e. g. in prisons or the armed forces. Sometimes there will be no or not enough people to offer spiritual care, especially very small religious communities may have problems in this respect.

---

49 Vertr. zw. d. Bundesrep. Deutschland u. d. Zentralrat d. Juden in Deutschland z. Regelung d. jüdischen Militärseelsorge (JüdMilSeelsVtr) v. 20.12.2019 (BGBl. 2020 I p. 1665).

50 So Vertr. Bad.-Württ./Israelit. Rel.gem. (note 27), art. 3 & Schlussprot.; Staatsvertr. Berlin / Jüd. Gem. (note 27), art. 3; Vertr. Brandenb./Jüd. Gem. (note 27), art. 3; Vertr. Hamburg / Jüd. Gem. (note 27), art. 5 & Protokollerkl. zu art. 5 sec. 2.

51 Vertr. Hamb./Alevit. Gem. (note 28), art. 7 & Prot.erkl.; Vertr.Rheinl.-Pf./Alevit. Gem. (note 28), art. 7.

52 *Schulten*, Anstaltsseelsorge für Muslime, KuR, 20 (2014), 50–66 (55 ss.).

VII. Churches and chapels in prisons, hospitals, army barracks, airports

In many army barracks, hospitals and prisons there are churches and chapels because the people living and working in these institutions cannot or may not leave. Because the Federal Republic or its member states are the owners of the properties in question, they have to build, maintain and normally also to decorate the churches and chapels,[53] if there is no specific treaty with different regulations. But because the secular state and its departments are not allowed to make any specifications regarding religion and its rules, customs and proper liturgy, only the religious communities can decide, how the church or chapel has to be decorated.[54] The state may claim, that the working order of the institution as well as the budget for the building project is to be observed. If there are different religious communities, which have to use the same room, the state has to decide how to do it, weighing and balancing all the different positions as best as possible. Only if the church or chapel is classified as a historical monument, the state may demand, that the principles of historic preservation are observed.[55]

VIII. Conclusion

Spiritual care in Germany has various legal foundations: the constitutions of the Federal Republic and its member states, treaties between state and churches and religious communities, laws and administrative agreements protect and form it. So, it is well guaranteed for the future. Today spiritual care is a part of a wide range of forms of specialized care, which all try to help people in situations of distress. The secular state cooperates with churches and religious communities to provide spiritual care in its institutions, because it supports the fundamental freedoms of its citizens including the freedom of faith and religion. The state may not identify with a specific religion or religion as such, so it must guarantee, that spiritual care is always voluntary, and it may not determine the religious content of spiritual care – that is strictly the affair of the religious communities. Spiritual care is not only a part of religious freedom (art. 4 sec. 1,2 GG) it is also protected by the guarantee of human dignity (art. 1 sec. 1 GG) – so it must be ensured in every social and liberal state in Germany forever.

---

53 Explicit: Vertr. Hl. Stuhl/Sachsen (note 25), Schlußprot. zu art. 12 sec. 1.

54 Cf. note 42, 48 and BVerfG KirchE 48, 398 = DVBl 2007, 119 – Mun.

55 Look for details: *Hammer*, Kirchenbauten in Staatseigentum unter d. Grundgesetz und kirchl. Veränderungs- u. Umgestaltungswünsche hieran, in: *Muckel* (ed.), Kirche und Religion im sozialen Rechtsstaat. Festschrift für Wolfgang Rüfner zum 70. Geburtstag, 2003, p. 159–176.

Religious Assistance in Spain
Some Notes with Special Attention to the Condition of Migrants

BEATRICE SERRA

I. Introduction

In this article, religious assistance is understood as the activity carried out by the State to meet the religious needs of internees in centers characterized by a special regime of subjection.[1]

That said, this contribution aims to analyze the Spanish system of religious assistance with specific attention to two contexts in which migrants alone or also benefit from this assistance: detention centers for foreigners and prison facilities.

The focus on the condition of migrants is justified by the link that exists today in Spain between the management of the religious dimension and the management of the migratory phenomenon, to the point that many choices on the forms of exercising the right to religious freedom have been made within the framework of public policies on immigration.[2] And this for at least two reasons: 1) because in the 21st century Spain has hosted more than five million foreigners, transforming itself from a country of emigrants to a country that welcomes migrants with the consequent problem of the political, economic and social management of diversity; 2) because attention to the religion of migrants is of great importance for their integration in the host country and for the peaceful coexistence of a multicultural and multi-religious society such as Spanish society.

---

1 For this essential notion of religious assistance see: *Payá Rico,* Asistencia religiosa en centros de internamimento de extranjeros. Revision de los convenios de colaboración: realidad y sugerencias, in Anuario de Derecho Eclesiástico del Estado 2021, p. 293–294.

2 On this aspect see: *Camarero Suárez/Reguart Segarra,* Las migraciones y su impacto en el progreso de la libertad religiosa en España e Italia: contraste de ordeniamentos, 2023, Navarra, p. 19–34.

II. Religious assistance in the Spanish legal system: general profiles

In Spain, the provision by the State of a system of religious assistance is a direct consequence of the fundamental right of religious freedom enshrined in Article 16.1 of the Spanish Constitution of 1978. This article, read together with Article 9.2 of the same Constitution, which enshrines the obligation of the public authorities to act for the realization of the principle of formal and substantial equality, configures religious freedom as a positive freedom, the defense of which requires active action by the State.

Well, for the realization of the right to religious freedom, positive action by the State is particularly necessary precisely when the person has difficulty exercising this right because he or she is in a segregating or separate structure.

It is no coincidence that Organic Law No. 7/1980 of 5 July on Religious Freedom states in Article 2.1b) that the right of a person to receive religious assistance from the denomination to which he or she belongs is part of the scope of protection of the right to religious freedom.

The same Law, in Article 2.3, states that, for the real and effective application of the faculties deriving from the right to religious freedom, the Spanish public authorities must adopt the necessary measures to facilitate religious assistance in public military, hospital, welfare, penitentiary and other institutions dependent on them, as well as religious education in public educational centers.

Religious assistance, therefore, must be aimed at guaranteeing individuals in a segregating facility the exercise of the essential faculties envisaged in Article 2 of the Organic Law on Religious Freedom: the practice of acts of worship, the commemoration of feast days, the celebration of marriage rites, dignified burial without discrimination on religious grounds, religious instruction and information of all kinds, and meetings for religious purposes.

Unilateral regulations on religious assistance are flanked by bilateral regulations, the result of cooperation agreements between the Spanish State and the Holy See, the Federation of Evangelical Religious Bodies of Spain, the Federation of Jewish Communities of Spain, the Islamic Commission of Spain.[3] Agreements approved by ordinary laws implemented by subsequent administrative acts.[4]

However, neither the Constitution, nor Organic Law No. 5/1980 of 5 July defines a concrete form in which religious assistance is to be organized. It follows that any organizational model can be adopted.

---

3 For the Agreements between the Spanish State and religious denominations on spiritual assistance, see: *Moreno*, La asistencia religiosa en España, in *Martín Sánchez / Navarro Floria (ed.)*, La libertad religiosa en España y Argentina, 2006, Madrid, p. 99–119.

4 On this point, see: *Rodríguez Blanco*, Los convenios entre las administraciones pública y las confesiones religiosas, Pamplona, 2003.

In this regard, doctrine has identified four main models: the "organic integration" model, which configures the minister of religion entrusted with providing religious assistance as an official of the State; the "contractual or concerted relationship" model, which provides for the stipulation of a contract between the minister of religion and the segregating structure without charges for the religious denomination to which the minister of religion belongs, or an Agreement between the religious denomination and the State Administration; the "free access" model, according to which the State guarantees ministers of religion access to the segregating structure, but does not bear the relative financial burden; the "freedom of exit" model, according to which those interned in public centers are authorized to go to the places of worship of the religious denomination they belong to in order to participate in sacred rites.[5]

The choice between these models is conditioned by the type of segregating structure, but, above all, by the principles that govern relations between the State and the religious factor. In this sense, two closely connected principles, enshrined (directly or indirectly) in the Spanish Constitution, appear to be decisive: the principle of the secularity of the State, which excludes any identification between the State and the religious sphere, and the principle of cooperation with religious denominations (Art. 16.3), the latter also understood as a means of promoting the freedom and equality of individuals and groups in religious matters (cf. Art. 9. 2).[6]

Given these two principles (secularity and collaboration), the models of religious assistance that are most functional to any type of segregating structure and to the Spanish constitutional order are, therefore, the "contractual relationship or concertation" model and the "free access" model.

Less useful is the "freedom of exit" model, which cannot be applied, for example, to individuals detained in prison facilities, while the "organic integration" model, historically present in the Spanish reality, has been progressively superseded due to its uncertain compatibility with the non-confessional character of the State[7].

Certainly, although the Spanish State has the task of providing all the necessary measures so that those in a segregating structure can exercise the faculties deriving from the fundamental right of religious freedom, religious assistance is not a public service or an activity proper to the State but remains a matter for religious denominations.

---

5 On these models, see: *López Alarcón,* Asistencia religiosa, in *Ferrer Ortiz (coord.),* Derecho Eclesiástico del Estado Español, 1996, Pamplona, p. 308–310.

6 On this point, see: *Fernández- Coronado,* Sentido de la cooperación del Estado laico en una socieda multirreligiosa, in Revista General de Derecho Canónico y de Derecho Eclesiástico del Estado, 19, 2009, www.iustel.com (accessed 25 July 2025), p. 7, 18.

7 On this point, see *Mantecón Sancho,* La asistencia religiosa en el sistema penitenciario español, in Anuario de Derecho Eclesiástico del Estado, 1996, p. 239–245.

At the same time, the Spanish State must also guarantee religious assistance to those who, in segregated or separate facilities, do not identify with traditional religious denominations, but feel the need to have support consistent with their moral and philosophical convictions according to a broad concept of religion.

The objective of religious assistance is, therefore, the promotion of religious freedom and equality both between believers of different religious denominations and between believers and non-believers.

III. Religious assistance in foreigners' internment centers

Having outlined the basic lines of the Spanish religious assistance system, one can now verify how these lines are applied in the centers of internment for foreigners where mainly Islamic believers are present.

Internment centers for foreigners were established by the first Spanish immigration law: Organic Law No. 7 of 1985 on the rights and freedoms of foreigners in Spain, Article 26 of which provides for the possibility for the judge to decide on the entry of the foreigner into the detention center pending expulsion, repatriation or return.

The matter has been the subject of several amendments: the Order of the Ministry of the Presidency of 22 February 1999 on the rules of operation and internal regime of the centers; Organic Law n° 4/2000, of 11 January 2000, on the rights and freedoms of foreigners in Spain and on social integration and its reform by Organic Law n° 14/2003 of 20 November; Royal Decree n° 162/2004, of 14 March 2004, approving the Regulations on the operation and internal regime of Internment Centers for Foreigners.[8]

It follows from all of these rules that: a) Internment centers for foreigners are public establishments of a non-penitentiary nature under the authority of the Ministry of the Interior, intended to detain and hold foreigners who do not meet the necessary requirements to enter Spanish territory and must remain there for more than 72 hours before they can be returned to their countries of origin or who, having their legal residence in Spain, are subject to expulsion proceedings from the national territory for one of the reasons provided for in Organic Law no. 4 of 11 January 2000 or Article 89 of the Penal Code; b) entry to the centers is an exceptional and subsidiary measure that has exclusively a preventive and precautionary purpose; c) internees are restricted in their freedom of movement, but there are no specific limitations on the other rights and freedoms that the Spanish legal system recognizes for foreigners.

---

8 For a commentary on this framework see: *Payá Rico*, (note 1), p. 288–290.

With regard specifically to religious freedom, while Art. 23. 2 of the Organic Law on the Rights and Freedoms of Foreigners prohibits discrimination on religious grounds, Art. 45 of the Regulations on the Operation and Internal Regime of Internment Centers for Foreigners, entitled "Religious Practice" enshrines the obligation of those who run the centers to: a) guarantee and respect the religious freedom of interned foreigners, facilitating the means for its practice; b) help foreigners comply with religious rules on food, feast days and rituals, consistent with the security needs of the center and the fundamental rights of other interned foreigners.

In concrete terms, after the entry into force of the Regulation on the functioning and internal regime of centers of internment for foreigners, the Ministry of the Interior, to guarantee religious practice in these centers, entered into a Cooperation Agreement with the Catholic Church of 12 June 2014 and three Cooperation Agreements with the Evangelical Church, Jewish Communities and Islamic Communities of 4 March 2015.[9]

These Agreements, which are administrative in nature, have the same structure and substantial content, with a real equality between the Catholic Church and other religious denominations, and do not provide for financial burdens on the State.

In addition to the specific modalities of religious assistance agreed in the Cooperation Agreements, in general terms, the model currently applied in Spanish centers for the internment of foreigners is that of free access, so that following a request from the internees, ministers of religion are authorized to go to the centers to provide religious assistance without ever violating the rules guaranteeing order and security. This model conforms to the principle of secularism, since ministers of religion are not incardinated in the State administration and can be applied to any religious denomination and in any detention facility. However, especially in detention centers for foreigners, the free-access model does not guarantee timely religious assistance, nor does it always allow this assistance to be well coordinated with the facility's other activities.

IV. Religious assistance in prison facilities

In prison facilities, religious assistance is of particular importance both because the condition of prisoners is one of subjection par excellence that does not allow a normal relationship with the outside world, and because religious belief has great relevance for the psychological serenity of subjects deprived of their liberty and

9 For the specific contents of these Agreements see: *Payá Rico*, (note 1), p. 303–311.

can contribute to the re-education and social reintegration of convicts as an objective of the Spanish prison system.[10]

The consideration of religious beliefs for the rehabilitation of inmates is perhaps even more relevant in the case of foreign inmates, who make up about one third of the Spanish prison population and belong mainly to the Evangelical Church and Islam.[11]

That being said, the right to receive religious assistance in prison finds its first legal basis in Article 25.2 of the Spanish Constitution, according to which anyone serving a prison sentence shall enjoy the fundamental rights provided for in Chapter Two, Title One, of the Constitution that are not expressly limited by the content of the sentence, the purpose of the sentence and prison law, and always without prejudice to the right to the full development of one's personality.

Consistent with the constitutional principle, Organic Law no. 1/1979, of 26 September, General Penitentiary Law, establishes: a) that prison life must be conducted with respect for the personality of inmates and their legal rights and interests not affected by punishment, without distinction of race, political opinion, religious belief, social condition (see art. 3); b) that the Administration must provide prisoners with controlled food, taking account, as far as possible, of their philosophical and religious convictions (see art. 21.2); c) that upon request prisoners may be authorized to communicate with priests or ministers of their religion (see art. 51.3); d) that the Administration must guarantee and facilitate the exercise of prisoners' religious freedom (see art. 54).

Similarly, Article 230 of Royal Decree No 190/1996 of 6 February, the Prison Regulations, establishes the right of prisoners to turn to a registered religious denomination to request religious assistance, provided that this is provided with respect for the rights of other persons.

This unilateral regulation on the protection of prisoners' religious freedom is flanked by regulations derived from the Convention.

As far as the Catholic Church is concerned, the Agreement on Juridical Affairs between the Spanish State and the Holy See of 3 January 1979 is of primary importance.

---

10 On religious assistance in the Spanish prison system in general, see: *Mantecón Sancho*, (note 7); *Rodríguez Blanco*, Asistencia religiosa penitenciaria de las confesiones minoritarias con Acuerdo de cooperación, in *Martín Sánchez, González Sánchez (ed.)*, Algunas cuestiones controvertidas del ejercicio del derecho fundamental de libertad religiosa en España, 2009, Madrid, p. 183–207; *Rodríguez Blanco*, La presencia de la religión en los establecimientos públicos como exigencia del derecho fundamental de libertad religiosa. El ejemplo de la asistencia religiosa en centros penitenciarios conforme al derecho internacional, in Anuario de Derecho Eclesiástico del Estado, 2015, p. 103–124.

11 On these aspects see: *Rodríguez Blanco*, Asistencia religiosa penitenciaria de las confesiones minoritarias con Acuerdo de Cooperación, p. 183–184.

Article IV of this Agreement, after recognizing the right to religious assistance of those in segregated facilities, obliges the Spanish State to agree with the competent authorities of the Church on the regime of Catholic religious assistance and the pastoral activities of priests and religious in prison facilities. Fulfilling this obligation, in 1993 the Agreement on Catholic Religious Assistance in Prison Institutions was signed by the President of the Spanish Episcopal Conference and the Spanish Minister of Justice.[12] Article 2 of this Agreement defines the content of Catholic religious assistance: the celebration of Holy Mass on religious holidays and optionally on any other day; visits to prisoners; religious instruction and training and listening to those who have doubts in religious or moral matters; the celebration of acts of worship and the administration of the sacraments; any activity directly related to the religious development of prisoners and the humanization of prison life.[13]

Catholic religious assistance is provided by priests appointed by the local Ordinary, who, even if formally authorized by the General Directorate of Penitentiary Institutions, do not belong to the State organization, with an explicit overcoming of the "organic integration" system, since religious assistance is no longer an activity of the detention facility. However, the economic burden of the service is borne by the State, which reimburses the dioceses, while the presence in each prison of a chapel or other suitable place of worship is provided for.

As far as non-Catholic religious assistance is concerned, the Cooperation Agreements of 12 November 1992 with the Federation of Evangelical Religious Bodies of Spain, the Federation of Jewish Communities of Spain and the Islamic Commission of Spain apply.

Article 9 of these Agreements sanctions the right to religious assistance for inmates in public facilities; a right whose exercise is guaranteed by ministers permanently dedicated to worship, designated by the respective religious denominations and authorized by the corresponding facilities.

Ministers may access the facilities freely and without time limits and have the right to use premises to conduct religious services.

In any case, also to avoid undue proselytizing, the three Agreements state that religious assistance will be provided by ministers of religion in full respect of the principle of religious freedom and the rules of organization of the centers, including prison rules. This raises the problem of reconciling the security rules limiting the entrance of visitors to prisons with the right of ministers of religion to always access them.

---

12 On this point, see: *M. Moreno Antón,* La asistencia religiosa católica e centros penitenciarios. Comentario al Acuerdo de 20 de mayo de 1993 entre el Presidente de la CEE y el Ministro de Justicia, in Revista Española de Derecho Canónico, 1994, p. 199–216.

13 On the content of the 1993 Agreement see: *Mantecón Sancho,* (note7), p. 693–695.

As far as economic aspects are concerned, unlike what is provided for the Catholic Church, the Cooperation Agreements with the Evangelical and Jewish Communities establish that the expenses are to be borne by the religious denominations.

In the case of Islamic religious assistance, instead, a specific Cooperation Agreement between the State and the Islamic Commission of Spain of 24 October 2007 established that Islamic ministers of worship receive State financial support if their work is requested by at least 10 prisoners.

Prior to this Cooperation Agreement, moreover, the discipline on non-Catholic prison religious assistance was developed by Royal Decree No. 710/2006, which defined its content: religious and moral instruction and counselling; funeral rites; worship on public holidays or other days for justified reasons, always in compliance with the prison operating rules.[14]

Certainly, it emerges from what has been said so far that in Spanish prisons, among the non-Catholic confessions, Islamic religious assistance is the one that enjoys the most favorable regime.

However, even this scheme presents at least two problems, highlighted by the Islamic Commission. The first is that the State's financial contribution is often insufficient to cover the travel expenses of ministers of religion to prison centers.

The second and more serious problem is cultural. In fact, the exercise of Islamic beliefs is considered a potential radicalizing factor. As a result, a Muslim detainee who asks to receive religious assistance is often subjected to special monitoring, which induces him to renounce exercising his right to religious assistance and to live his detention by hiding his faith.[15]

V. Brief conclusions

Consideration of the Spanish system of religious assistance, and in particular the system of religious assistance provided for migrant internment centers and penal institutions, allows us to verify the protection of religious freedom in a European country characterized by a strong cultural and religious pluralism due to the phenomenon of migration.

Certainly, in Spain, the realization of the principle of secularism has led to the passage from the historical model of "organic integration" to the model of "consultation" and "free access", proper to a State that has equal relations with all religious

---

14 On these aspects see: *M. Rodríguez Blanco,* Asistencia religiosa penitenciaria de las confesiones minoritarias con Acuerdo de Cooperación, cit., p. 183–207.

15 On this aspect see: V. *Camarero Suárez, N. Reguart Segarra,* Las migraciones y su impacto en el progreso de la libertad religiosa en España e Italia: contraste de ordeniamentos, cit., p. 40.

denominations. The Spanish reality demonstrates, therefore, that collaboration with religious confessions is the first instrument to guarantee everyone an effective exercise of the fundamental right to religious freedom in a secular and plural context.

However, the use of the principle of collaboration – so that specific agreements are needed to clearly and fully guarantee the right to religious assistance – is not fully satisfactory.

The ever-changing needs arising from a multicultural and multi-religious society require, in fact, a continuous and rapid updating of regulations, which cannot be tied to the stipulation of Cooperation Agreements that, moreover, do not protect those belonging to a religious denomination that has not entered into agreements with the State.

At the same time, there is the scarcity of Agreements on the financing of religious assistance and the fact that this assistance is only paid for by the State for the Catholic and Islamic religions and only in penal institutions.

Spiritual Care in Public Hospitals and Care Facilities in Austria*

ANDREAS KOWATSCH

I. Spiritual Care in Hospitals – Preliminary Remarks

Offering pastoral[1] care, especially in life-threatening circumstances, is part of the essential aspects of the Christian churches' mission.[2] However, caring for the sick is not a Christian phenomenon, but part of the ethics of most major religions. The hospital chaplaincy organized under the umbrella of the Islamic Religious Community in Austria,[3] for example, serves to fulfil a religious duty of Islam.[4] On behalf of the Chief Rabbinate of the Jewish Community of Vienna, two volunteer chaplains provide Jewish patient care at the General Hospital of the City of Vienna (AKH).[5] The Buddhist Religious Society is responsible for the service of Buddhist patient care.[6] For members of Jehovah's Witnesses, too, it is true that "not only the

---

* This paper is based on my detailed article "Religionsrechtliche Fragen der Krankenhausseelsorge in Österreich", in: *Rees/Kalb/Niemand* (eds.), Kanonist, Ordensmann und Gestalter: Festschrift zur Emeritierung von Univ.-Prof. Mag. theol. Dr. iur. Dr. iur. can. Severin Johann Lederhilger OPraem, 2023, Berlin, p. 517–551. It has been revised, updated and translated for this volume.

1 Even if the terms *pastoral care* and *spiritual care* are largely used synonymously in this article, it should be noted that spiritual care represents a more comprehensive concept of care and also transcends denominational boundaries. The resulting questions of religious law would require a separate study.

2 The reports of those affected in *Berghofer/Petritsch/Schwarz*, Was willst Du, dass ich Dir tue? (Lk 18:41). Zur Situation der katholischen Krankenhausseelsorge (KHS) Österreichs während der Covid-19-Pandemie, in: *Kröll et al. (eds.)*, Die Corona-Pandemie. Ethische, gesellschaftliche und theologische Reflexionen einer Krise, 2020, Baden-Baden (= Bioethik in Wissenschaft und Gesellschaft 10), p. 283–298.

3 German: Islamische Glaubensgemeinschaft in Österreich, abbr. IGGÖ.

4 See the information provided by the IGGÖ at: https://www.derislam.at/spitalseelsorge/ (accessed 25 July 2025). See also *Elsabagh/Elgendy*, Spiritualität im Krankenhaus aus der Sicht der islamischen Seelsorge, in: *Körtner et al. (eds.)*, Spiritualität, Religion und Kultur am Krankenbett, 2009, New York, p. 41–45.

5 *Weisz*, Zum Wohle des jüdischen Patienten im AKH Wien, in: *Körtner et al. (eds.)*, Spiritualität, Religion und Kultur am Krankenbett, 2009, Vienna, p. 36–40.

6 According to the brief self-presentation on www.akh-seelsorge.at/buddhistische-krankenbegleitung (accessed 25 July 2025), the focus is on the spiritual care of the deceased or the bereaved relatives.

body needs to be cared for".[7] As pastoral care for the sick is often not possible at home or in buildings dedicated to religious purposes, pastoral care workers are dependent on access to those facilities that are set up to care for the sick and dying.[8]

Chaplains who come to the hospital from outside enter a highly complex organization into which they have to fit. The possible spectrum of experiences they can make ranges from rejection and indifference to an open-hearted welcome in the shared service of the sick. Even where a healthcare facility has its own institutionalized pastoral care, the acceptance of the non-medical services of pastoral care in relation to doctors and nurses and those in many other professions in the hospital context must always be worked out anew. As people from all backgrounds come together in the hospital to provide services and seek help, the hospital is a mirror of a pluralistic society and its diverse, even contradictory concepts of meaning. Hospital chaplains and their staff inevitably find themselves in a "sitting on the fence" situation.[9] They are integrated into the hospital institution with its own rules,[10] which can also take different forms depending on the hospital. Hospital chaplaincy itself is therefore caught between the self-image of the religious community in whose name it works and the plurality of religious expectations. It is aimed at the patients but must also have the hospital staff in mind. Pastoral care is carried out in the name of the religious community and at the same time depends entirely on the person of the chaplain. It is aimed at the members of the respective community. These may have very different needs with regard to religious care even if they are formal adherents. Due to the individual aspect of the right to religious freedom, these needs can also be hostile to pastoral care. There are many areas of overlap between the protection of religious freedom under corporate and individual law, but they are not necessarily congruent.

Territorially organized pastoral care is supplemented by the services of "categorical" pastoral care. In a narrower sense, this is there to make religious life possible for people in situations in which they are unable to participate in the life of their congregation or association for particular reasons. Prisoners, for example, are not able to attend church services in their congregation. Members of the military and its institutions are subject to various restrictions. The radius of movement of the sick is often restricted to the hospital or nursing home, and there often only to

---

7 See the website about the pastoral care for the sick of the Religious Society of Jehovah's Witnesses in Austria www.krankenseelsorge.at (accessed 25 July 2025).

8 For the history of pastoral care in hospitals, see *Klessmann*, Von der Krankenseelsorge zur Krankenhausseelsorge – historische Streiflichter, in: *Roser (ed.)*, Handbuch der Krankenhausseelsorge, 5th edn. 2019, Göttingen, p. 34–41.

9 On the "in-between" as a definition of the place of hospital pastoral care, see *Klessmann*, Die Fremdheit und Widerständigkeit der Seelsorge im Krankenhaus, in: *Roser* (note 8), p. 391–401.

10 It is obvious that business logic and constraints are also part of these inherent laws. See *Haart*, Die Rolle der Seelsorge im Wirtschaftsunternehmen Krankenhaus, in: *Roser* (note 8), p. 92–103.

their own bed, so that without the access of chaplains to these facilities, religious life would be endangered precisely in a situation where the sick person could draw healing potential from their own faith.

II. Hospital Chaplaincy from a Religious Law Perspective

II.1 Hospital Chaplaincy in the Tension Between the Freedom of Religious Communities and the Religious Freedom of Individuals

Art. 15 of the Austrian State Basic Law (StGG) from 1867 grants all legally recognized churches and religious societies the right to independently organize and administer their internal affairs. Insofar as the doctrine of a religious society includes outreach to the sick as part of its own mission, the right to self-determination would come to nothing if the "administration", i. e. the exercise of pastoral care, were made impossible by legal measures or de facto obstacles.[11]

However, pastoral care for the sick is not just a right of the churches and religious societies as institutions. Rather, the focus is on the sick and dying themselves. Even during a temporary or even permanent stay in a healthcare facility, they (naturally) remain subject to the fundamental right to freedom of religion, which in Austria is constitutionally standardized in Art. 14 of the StGG 1867, Art. 63 par. 2 of the Treaty of St. Germain and in Art. 9 of the ECHR.[12] Even if the Austrian legal system – apart from the "building laws" of the constitution secured by Art. 44 par. 3 of the Austrian Federal Constitution Act (B-VG) – does not know gradations within the category of federal constitutional law, the multiple guarantees of religious freedom and the context of their respective regulation show the special significance of this fundamental right. In view of the religiously and ideologically neutral character of the liberal constitutional state, this significance takes on a special freedom-securing meaning in comparison to its historical origins in the constitutional monarchy with its system of "Staatskirchenhoheit".

The positive freedom of religion of the individual is based on the right to one's own religious conviction as freedom of conscience. The exercise of religious belief is often linked to membership of a religious community. The criteria that determine this affiliation go beyond the realm of personal conscience. However, it is also not within the competence of the ideologically and religiously neutral state to determine them but is part of the core area of internal affairs. In order to guarantee

11 On the question of the extent to which the exercise of hospital chaplaincy is made more difficult by data protection law, see below, IV.
12 Art. 10 CFR also applies to the implementation and enforcement of Union law.

this right, the state also has a duty to shape the legal system in such a way that the practice of religion is not hindered for no reason.

For the state sector, negative religious freedom means that it must be possible at any time to terminate an affiliation established under religious law by leaving the religious community. However, as long as a person belongs to a religious community of their own free will, there is a presumption on the one hand that their formal affiliation and their own inner beliefs coincide to such an extent that religious offers made by their own community are accepted. On the other hand, the fundamental right to freedom of religion also protects the individual's decision not to make use of a religious offering from their own community and to contradict the content of the guidelines of their own religious community.[13] The fact that not only non-religious people and members of other religious communities, but also members of their own community can invoke the negative aspect of religious freedom is not undermined by the corporate freedom of the religious community. However, since in the case of members of a religion who reject the services of their own community, there is an objective difference between a person's affiliation to a particular religion and their (negative) confession, both of which are based on the same free will, the rejection must be made known to the outside world.[14] An insinuation, that the members reject the pastoral care of their own community as long as they have not actively asked for it, amounts to the assumption of a divided will. However, where individuals refuse pastoral care of their own accord, this must be respected. It follows that the provision of pastoral care in general does not depend on a patient's expressed wish, but only the provision of pastoral care to a particular patient.

---

13 In the ruling VfSlg. 15.592/1999, the Constitutional Court VfGH states: "Irrespective of the formal criteria of belonging to a particular religious community, 'one's own confession' is the outward declaration of inner (religious) attitudes and values; it cannot therefore be equated with formal membership." Specifically, the question was whether a prisoner who has not yet been accepted into the religious community of Jehovah's Witnesses may, at his request, receive pastoral care from a representative of this religious community. This presupposes that the religious representative is willing to comply with this request.

14 Probably the best-known example of this is the possibility of deregistration from denominational religious education. As long as this is not done in accordance with the legal requirements, religious education is a compulsory subject.

II.2 Hospital Chaplaincy in the Concordat and in Various Recognition Acts

a) In the Concordat of 1933/34

In Art. XVI of the Austrian Concordat (ÖK),[15] which in Austria's current legal system has the status of a simple federal law in addition to being binding under international law,[16] the Republic undertakes to guarantee the right of free access to the inmates of public hospitals, sanatoriums, nursing homes and similar institutions for the responsible chaplain to freely exercise his spiritual ministry. This right can only be denied if, in agreement with the respective diocesan bishop, the institution concerned has established its own structures of pastoral care.

If this is not the case, the determination of who is the responsible pastor is based on the internal church regulations. The corresponding standardization constitutes an internal matter pursuant to Art. 15 of the StGG, so that a refusal of access on the grounds that the person concerned is not competent to provide pastoral care in the specific case would only be admissible if an obviously incompetent person were to invoke the Concordat or an obviously non-existent appointment by the Church. Where there is no institutional integration of Catholic pastoral care in the healthcare facility in question, the primary responsibility lies with the patient's priest of residence.[17] Since in many cases, especially in larger cities, there is no connection to the parish of residence, the priest in whose parish the hospital is located can also be considered as the "responsible pastor".[18]

The administration of communion to the sick as a means of strengthening and the anointing of the sick are expressly standardized in canon law as official duties of pastors (c. 911 § 1 CIC[19] and c. 922 CIC). As a minimum measure of corporate freedom, the Church claims that the sacramental pastoral care of the sick can be practiced unhindered.

---

15 Concordat between the Holy See and the Republic of Austria including additional protocol StF: Federal Law Gazette II No. 2/1934 as amended by Federal Law Gazette No. 195/1960.

16 In the state order of the years before the annexation of Austria to the National Socialist German Reich, some articles had constitutional status. *Schima*, Overestimated by friend and foe? Das österreichische Konkordat 1933/34, in: *Reiter-Zatloukal/Rothländer/Schölnberger (eds.)*, Österreich 1933–1938. Interdisziplinäre Annäherungen an das Dollfuß-Schuschnigg-Regime, 2012, Vienna-Cologne-Weimar, p. 42–57 (47).

17 C. 529 § 1 CIC standardizes the ministerial duty of the pastor to assist the sick, especially the dying, with devoted love by carefully strengthening them through the sacraments and commending their souls to God.

18 As soon as a patient establishes at least a quasi-residence (c. 102 CIC) in the hospital or care facility, the local pastor of the hospital also becomes the patient's own pastor.

19 In addition to parish priests, parochial vicars, chaplains and superiors of a community in clerical religious institutes or societies of apostolic life are also named there for all those who reside in the house. "Chaplains" within the meaning of c. 911 CIC are priests who are appointed for the categorical pastoral care of the sick. See cc. 564–566 CIC.

Art. XVI of the ÖK does not grant the responsible chaplain a directly enforceable subjective right of access. However, the Republic undertakes to guarantee this access, which entails the obligation to enact corresponding legal provisions in hospital law. Here, the Concordat concretizes the state's obligation to guarantee access already (at least indirectly) contained in Art. 15 of the StGG.[20] Under international law, the Concordat obliges the Republic and thus the federal government and the federal states.

According to the wording of the treaty, Art. XVI of the ÖK ensures access to the institutions mentioned therein in order to enable the pastor to exercise his spiritual ministry. Systematically, the contracting parties thus focus on the institutional safeguarding of the Church's mission in special situations in which unhindered contact between the pastor and the faithful is not readily possible. However, enabling the exercise of spiritual ministry is aimed at the pastoral care of the faithful who find themselves in a situation of limited mobility. In essence, the concordat provision therefore also safeguards the exercise of patients' individual religious freedom.

b) Sec. 18 of the Act on External Legal Relationships of the Protestant Church (Protestant Act)

The Protestant Act (ProtG),[21] which came into force in 1961, is characterized in several respects by the fact that it serves as a model among religious recognition laws. At the same time, it is generally regarded as the most freedom-sensitive standardization of the external legal relationships of a recognized religious society.

Both observations apply in particular to Sec. 18 of the Protestant Act. Both Sec. 7 par. 1 of the Act on Oriental Churches (OrthodoxG 1967)[22] and Sec. 3 par. 1 of the Act on Ancient Oriental Churches (OrientKG 2003)[23] refer to this provision, which is why it can be considered a central norm of hospital chaplaincy law.

---

20 *Potz*, Recht auf seelsorgliche Betreuung aus der Sicht der Patienten und der Religionsgemeinschaften, in: *Körtner et al. (eds.)*, Spiritualität, Religion und Kultur am Krankenbett, 2009, Vienna, p. 108–118 (109).

21 Federal law of 6 July 1961 on the External Legal Relations of the Protestant Church, original version: Federal Law Gazzette No. 182/1961. The term "Protestant Act" raises no questions of political correctness in Austria and is also used by the Church herself.

22 Federal Act of 23 June 1967 on the External Legal Relations of the Greek-Oriental Church in Austria, original version: Federal Law Gazette No. 229/1967 as amended by Federal Law Gazette I No. 68/2011.

23 Federal Act on External Legal Relations of the Oriental Orthodox Churches in Austria (Oriental Orthodox Church Act; OrientKG), Federal Law Gazette I No. 20/2003.

In terms of content, Sec. 18 of the ProtG guarantees, directly or by reference, the Protestant, Orthodox and Ancient Oriental Churches the exercise of pastoral care for their members who are accommodated in public hospitals, nursing homes and similar institutions by ministers authorized and designated by the respective church.

Sec. 18 of the ProtG also has a model character for the institutional placement of pastoral care in hospitals. Insofar as no separate pastoral care for the sick has been established, according to par. 3 1st sentence leg. cit., the minister appointed and designated by the respective church must be given free access to the sick belonging to his Church. The "free exercise" of pastoral care must also be made possible. The internal hospital regulations must stipulate that the chaplain must be informed whether and which believers have been admitted. In the event of imminent danger, the chaplain must be informed immediately (par. 3 2nd sentence leg. cit).

The prerequisite for this information is that the patient's religious confession is queried in the course of admission to the facility. Due to the negative freedom of religion, this information must be voluntary. If no information is provided by the patient, it must be implicitly assumed that the patient does not wish to make use of the hospital's pastoral care services. Religious acts towards persons whose religious denomination is unknown must be avoided. The mere provision of information about the services offered by the hospital chaplaincy is not prohibited, as on the one hand the mere failure to provide information about one's religious beliefs cannot be construed as an active rejection of any contact of a general nature, and on the other hand it cannot be assumed that a patient would not be able to change his or her mind in the course of a sometimes lengthy stay. The Church's right to information standardized in the Protestant Act therefore only applies to persons who have made their affiliation to the Protestant Church known. However, the Church's right to information raises data protection issues that could not yet be considered at the time the Protestant Act was enacted.[24]

Although chaplains are free in matters of religious care, they must integrate themselves into the institutional structure. Accordingly, Sec. 18 par. 4 of the ProtG stipulates that they must observe the provisions of the institutional regulations when exercising their function and follow the orders of the competent institutional bodies in matters that do not concern spiritual matters. Insofar as there is no employment relationship with the hospital, the Church remains responsible for disciplinary measures, whereby the hospital management may exercise its domestic authority in the event of imminent danger.

---

24 See below, IV.

c) The Islam Act of 2015

The legal recognition of followers of Islam "according to the Hanafi rite" by the Islam Act of 1912[25] created an innovative integration of Islam into the national religious law system compared to other European countries.[26] However, the original Islam Act had a number of regulatory gaps (and loopholes), which were to be remedied by the new version of the Islam Act in 2015. One of the gaps concerned the lack of an explicit[27] provision on pastoral care in institutions and therefore also in hospitals.

Probably for reasons of religious-political sensitivity, the Islam Act 2015 does not refer to Sec. 18 of the Protestant Act but standardizes an independent framework law for pastoral care in institutions. As pastoral care in institutions does not concern the right of recognition as such, which is regulated in the first two sections of the Islam Act 2015, a separate standardization was made for the IGGÖ (Sec. 11 par. 1 no. 3) and for the Alevi Religious Community in Austria in (Sec. 18 par. 1 no. 3 of the Islam Act).[28] If one compares both standards of the Islam Act with Sec. 18 of the Protestant Act, the Islam Act focuses more intensively on the person of the pastoral worker. Pursuant to Sec. 11 par. 2 and Sec. 18 par. 2 of the Islam Act only persons who are professionally and personally suitable for this due to their training and their place of residence in Austria may be considered as chaplains. Like Christian chaplains, they are solely responsible to the religious community in all religious ("denominational") matters, but to the respective management responsible for the institution in all other matters.

The more detailed definition of professional suitability is problematic under constitutional law. For this, a degree from an Austrian university institution for Islamic theology or an equivalent qualification is required. The assessment of per-

---

25 Original version: Imperial Law Gazette l No. 159/1912; after the deletion of the phrase "according to Hanafite rites" in force until 2015 as the Law of 15.07.1912, concerning the recognition of the followers of Islam as a religious society, Federal Law Gazette No. 164/1988. On the history of the Islam Act 1912, *Potz,* Das Islamgesetz 1912 und der religionsrechtliche Diskurs in Österreich zu Beginn des 20. Jahrhunderts, in: *Olechowski/Neschwara/Lengauer (eds.),* Grundlagen der österreichischen Rechtskultur, Festschrift Werner Ogris zum 75. Geburtstag, 2010, Vienna, p. 385–407.

26 See *Pabel,* Das Islamgesetz in rechtsvergleichender Perspektive, in: *Hinghofer-Szalkay/Kalb (eds.),* Islam, Recht und Diversität, 2018, Vienna, p. 341–354.

27 However, Sec. 6 contained an explicit affirmation of the principle of parity: "The religious society of the followers of Islam enjoys the same legal protection as other legally recognized religious societies as such as well as with regard to its religious practice and its religious servants." Of course, a complete ban on Islamic hospital chaplaincy would already have been unconstitutional on the basis of Art. 7 B-VG. In addition to the institutional guarantee and the right of recognition, however, even before 2015 it was not possible to deny visits to individual patients without violating their freedom to practice their religion.

28 Both provisions are worded identically: "The religious society has the right to provide religious care for its members who are accommodated in public hospitals, care, nursing or similar institutions."

sonal suitability is also not left to the religious communities alone but is made dependent on at least three years of relevant professional experience and knowledge of German at A-level. This provision overlooks the fact that hospital chaplaincy can also be carried out by volunteers according to the self-image of a religious society.[29] The obligation to have an academic degree in theology ignores the fact that pastoral care of the sick is not at the heart of the curricula of university studies and that, in addition to theological knowledge, it requires a range of at least equally important practical skills in conducting discussions, which are also not the subject of academic teaching. Both regulations interfere with the internal affairs of the religious communities concerned and, in their generality, violate[30] Art. 15 of the StGG.[31]

d) Jewish hospital chaplaincy

The Jewish Religious Society (Israelitische Religionsgesellschaft), which is a corporation under public law pursuant to Sec. 1 of the IsraelitenG[32] consists of religious communities (Kultusgemeinden) pursuant to Sec. 5 par. 1 of the IsraelitenG, whose task it is to ensure that the religious needs of their members are met and that the necessary facilities are provided. The religious communities, as independ-

---

29 See for example the criteria for the selection, training, commissioning and quality assurance of volunteers in the guidelines for hospital chaplaincy in the Archdiocese of Vienna, Das Profil der röm.-kath. Krankenhaus- und Pflegeheimseelsorge in der Erzdiözese Wien, 2008, Vienna, 8.

30 It cannot be ruled out that the state standardizes framework conditions for the professional and personal suitability of chaplains. However, these should not stipulate any theological requirements and should apply equally to all religious communities. The fact that knowledge of German is required may be desirable in terms of integration policy. However, in the context of pastoral care at the patient's bedside, it is crucial that patients are addressed in the language they speak. For communication with the other professional groups working in the hospital and with the management, knowledge of German is of course a prerequisite for the integration of pastoral care into the complex world of the hospital.

31 See the guidelines on pastoral care in hospitals of the Austrian catholic Pastoral Commission, Seelsorge im Krankenhaus (2000), www.pastoral.at/dl/NKOOJKJKKOKkLJqx4KJK/Seelsorge_im_Krankenhaus_pdf (accessed 23 September 2025), 15. Even if the text has no legal force under canon law, as a text of the Austrian Pastoral Commission it is an ecclesiastical perception of an internal matter. The requirements for the profession of hospital chaplain are therefore: personal aptitude, theological training (not necessarily a full degree in theology), special hospital chaplaincy training, a willingness to reflect on one's work and a willingness to undertake further training.

32 Law of 21 March 1890, concerning the regulation of the external legal relationships of the Israelite religious society, originally promulgated in: Imperial Lae Gazette No. 57/1890, fundamentally amended in Federal Law Gazette I No. 48/2012 as amended by Federal Law Gazette. I No. 166/2020.

ent public corporations, are therefore the organizational structures that bear responsibility for pastoral care of the sick within the Israelite Religious Society.[33]

Sec. 8 of the IsraelitenG specifies Art. 15 of the StGG as the right of the religious society to provide religious care in special institutions. In addition to members of the armed forces and persons in custody, this right also exists in accordance with par. 1 no. 3 in respect of its own members who are accommodated in public hospitals, care, nursing or similar institutions. While the costs for the religious care of members of the armed forces pursuant to par. 3 leg. cit. are borne by the federal government, the IsraelitenG does not contain any financial regulations concerning pastoral care in hospitals. In this respect, it does not differ from the other recognition laws.

A look at the religious recognition laws has shown that hospital chaplaincy is well established. However, hospital operators normally do not conduct their business in accordance with religious law, which is more or less foreign to many. Whether hospital chaplaincy can succeed without obstacles depends in particular on the status given to it by hospital law.

III. Hospital Chaplaincy and Hospital Law

III.1 1 Federal Act on Hospitals and Health Resorts (KAKuG)

Pursuant to Art. 12 par. 1 no. 1 of the Austrian Federal Constitution Act (B-VG), the federal legislator has the competence to enact basic laws in matters relating to sanatoriums and nursing homes, which serve as the basis for the enactment of implementing laws by the federal states. The provinces are subsequently responsible for implementation. In exercising this competence, the Federal Act on Hospitals and Health Resorts (KAKuG)[34] was enacted as early as 1957. The explicit emphasis on patients' rights in the KAKuG was made in the 1993 amendment.[35]

In accordance with the character of a basic law, Sec. 5a par. 1 no. 5 obliges the provincial legislators to oblige the providers of hospitals to ensure that pastoral care is available at the request of the "patient". The provision is embedded between no. 4, according to which it must be ensured that there are sufficient opportunities for visits and contact with the outside world, and no. 6, according to which psy-

---

33 On the Jewish tradition of *bikkur cholim* as non-medical psychosocial support, see *Probst (ed.)*, Die Begleitung Kranker und Sterbender im Judentum. Bikkur Cholim, jüdische Seelsorge und das jüdische Verständnis von Medizin und Pflege, 2017, Leipzig.

34 Federal Law on Hospitals and Health Resorts (KAKuG), original version: Federal Law Gazette No. 1/1957, last amended by Federal Law Gazette l. I No. 79/2022.

35 Federal Law Gazette No. 801/1993.

chological support must be provided at the request of the patient. The institutional location of pastoral care is therefore in the area of maintaining and safeguarding mental health.

A certain restriction arises from the fact that all of these measures must be provided by the hospital operators "in compliance with the purpose of the institution and the services offered". In any case, a constitutional interpretation in the light of religious freedom prohibits the complete prohibition of pastoral care services on the basis of structural arguments.

III.2 Patients Charter

Although patients' fundamental rights, civil law claims, subjective rights rooted in administrative law, social insurance claims and the protection of essential legal interests under criminal law were already standardized individually, a codification of patients' rights has been discussed since the early 1990s. On the one hand, such a codification was intended to make the scattering of individual rights due to competence law more manageable; on the other hand, the role of the patient as a subject and not merely as an object of medical action was to be strengthened by creating greater clarity.

Following the amendment of the KAKuG, an agreement between the federal government and the province of Carinthia pursuant to Art. 15a of the B-VG[36] formed a first step towards[37] a charter of patients' rights ("Patients Charter" – PC) that is equally binding for the federal government and the individual provinces.[38]

The Patients Charter summarizes the essential patient rights in four groups: the right to treatment and care, the right to patient dignity, the right to self-determination and the right to information and documentation.[39] As an agreement pursuant to Art. 15a of the Federal Constitutional Law, the Charter does not directly establish subjective rights for individuals, but obliges the parties involved in the agreement to implement what has been agreed in their respective areas of competence.

As a bracket over the rights codified below, Art. 2 of the PC stipulates that patients' individual rights must be particularly protected and that their human dig-

36 Federal Law Gazette I No. 195/1999.

37 Further bilateral agreements between the federal government and individual countries successively followed.

38 For the Province of Vienna: Agreement on safeguarding patients' rights (Patients Charter), StF: BGBl. I No. 42/2006.

39 Final provisions on the rights of children still need to be added.

nity must be respected and preserved under all circumstances.[40] The dignity and integrity of patients are to be expressly protected by the rights standardized in Section III (Art. 9–15) of the PC.[41]

The right to pastoral care is regulated in Art. 12 of the PC. This provision states: "The religious care of hospitalized patients shall be made possible at their request." The Patients Charter thus draws two boundaries: Only hospitalized patients should be entitled to this right and the right depends on the patient expressing a corresponding wish. The limitation to inpatients appears to be too narrow in view of the protective purpose. Patients receiving outpatient treatment may also find themselves in crisis situations, for example after being informed by a doctor of an unexpected diagnosis, which make religious care appear appropriate. The link between the patient's wishes and religious care should not obscure the fact that religious communities enjoy the right to offer pastoral care in hospitals irrespective of a specific patient's wishes. Without safeguarding the corporate aspect of religious freedom, individual wishes could not be met.

In addition to the right to religious care in the narrower sense, Art. 14 and 15 of the PC are also relevant to the exercise of pastoral care in hospitals. Patients undergoing inpatient care have the right to receive visits and maintain other contacts (Art. 14 par. 1 PC). This also includes visits and contacts with representatives of the patient's own religious community. At the same time, a patient's wish not to receive visitors or certain persons must be respected. The negative freedom of religion safeguards the patient's right to exclude pastors from the right to visit.

According to Art. 14 par. 2 of the PC, it must also be ensured that patients can name persons of trust who are to be informed in particular in the event of a sustained deterioration in their state of health and who are to be allowed contact with patients outside of visiting hours in such cases. Even if hospital chaplains are not explicitly mentioned, they undoubtedly belong to the group of possible confidants. In the context of legally exercised pastoral care, the offer to be available as such a person of trust is also possible. However, the decision to do so remains solely with the patient.

Art. 15 par. 1 of the PC requires measures to enable patients to die with dignity in inpatient facilities. As it is not possible to define this term universally, the situation of patients must be addressed as far as possible. For many religious people, the assistance of a chaplain in the immediate danger of death is part of a dignified death.

---

40 Human dignity as the highest guiding value of the entire legal system is not a concept of the Austrian Federal Constitution. However, human dignity and its protection are at least indirectly affirmed as the core of fundamental rights. However, the explicit reference to human dignity in the PC undoubtedly represents a major step forward for the liberal Austrian legal system.

41 However, the right to self-determination and information (Section IV PC) is also intrinsically linked to the protection of human dignity.

III.3 State Hospital Law

The basic provision of the KAKuG was implemented in the respective hospital laws of the nine Bundesländer (federal provinces). An examination of all these laws would exceed the scope of this article. The regulation of Lower Austria will therefore serve as an example.[42]

Sec. 16b par. 1 no. 5 of the Lower Austrian Hospitals Act (NÖ KAG)[43] obliges the legal entities of hospitals to ensure that pastoral care is available at the patient's request, taking into account the purpose of the institution and the services offered. The regulation is inserted between the right to visit and the right of access of a trusted person on the one hand and the right to psychological care at the patient's request on the other.

In addition to the patient's right to pastoral care, the Lower Austrian Hospital Act contains an explicit provision on the disclosure of patient data in a pastoral context.[44] According to Sec. 20 par. 3 NÖ KAG, the persons employed in the hospital can provide information on request in individual cases as to whether the patient has been admitted to the hospital and where they can be found. This regulation is intended to enable data protection-sensitive visits. This breach of the duty of confidentiality of employees is also expressly ordered for religious care. The patient retains the right to object to this provision of information. The objection can be limited to information provided to certain persons or only allow information to be provided to certain persons.

According to Sec. 6 par. 1 KuKAG, the internal operation of each hospital is regulated by the hospital's statute. The state legislature is responsible for deciding on the exact content of the hospital regulations, which are subject to the basic provisions of federal law. The hospital statutes must take particular account of patients' rights in all their provisions. The right of religious communities to provide pastoral care for the sick and the patient's right to religious care can be specified in the institutional regulations with regard to the specific institution. As the right to chaplains is enshrined in constitutional law, it can no more be excluded by institutional regulations than by ordinary legal measures.

---

42 For the eight other states´ laws, see the article I refer to under "*" at the beginning of this paper.

43 Lower Austrian Hospital Act (NÖ KAG), originally promulgated in: Federal State Law Gazette of Lower Austria, 9440-0 (WV), last amended by No. 49/2021.

44 In this important point, it differs from the other provincial laws.

IV. Hospital Chaplaincy and Data protection – A Multidimensional Fundamental Rights Issue

Between the institutional guarantees, the individual rights of patients and hospital law, there is a tension-filled structure that cannot be resolved unilaterally in favour of the individual patient's wishes or in favour of the smoothest possible organization of internal hospital processes without at the same time undermining the corporate right enshrined in constitutional law and guaranteed in the various religious recognition acts.

The logical prerequisite for churches and religious societies to be able to offer and perform their pastoral care services in a targeted manner, i. e. to their members, is that they first become aware that potential recipients of pastoral care are in a hospital. With regard to the corporate law aspect of the problem, Sec. 18 par. 3 2nd sentence of the ProtG interprets Art. 15 of the StGG consistently and standardizes the Church's right to information. If one acknowledges the principle of most-favoured treatment under religious law, this provision is at least also applicable to the other legally recognized religious communities. Since knowledge of the admission of one's own believers is a logical prerequisite for the exercise of (constitutionally) legally guaranteed rights, such a right is included in the special recognition laws, even if the respective wording is silent on the subject. The right of the IGGÖ and ALEVI to provide religious support to their members who are housed in the institutions listed therein, standardized in Sec. 11 par. 1 no. 3 and Sec. 18 par. 1 no. 3 of the Islam Act 2015, would come to nothing without knowledge of the whereabouts of the members. The same applies to the right of the Jewish Religious Community pursuant to Sec. 8 of the IsraelitenG.

However, the seemingly clear solution in terms of corporate religious freedom is overshadowed by the question of whether the legally mandated information in turn contradicts data protection law. According to reports, since the European General Data Protection Regulation 2018 – GDPR – came into force, smaller religious societies in particular have found themselves massively hindered in carrying out their mission towards their sick and dying members.[45]

The GDPR should establish a comparable level of data protection throughout the European Union. Union law takes precedence over all national law, including constitutional law.[46] Insofar as the GDPR contradicts Art. 15 of the StGG or le-

45 Former Protestant synod president Krömer even sees Protestant hospital chaplaincy as "dying"! See the report of 11.12.2019 on evang.at/synodenpraesident-kroemer-krankenhausseelsorge-ist-amsterben (accessed 25 July 2025).

46 This does not apply to the "building laws" of the Austrian Federal Constitution, as the people did not issue a blank check for total amendments to the Federal Constitution in the referendum on Austria's accession to the European Communities in 1995.

gal provisions on hospital chaplaincy, Union law takes precedence. Accordingly, the primacy of application also applies to the Concordat insofar as it is binding as a simple federal law.[47] However, a core area of the religious community's right to self-determination is also protected by Art. 9 of the ECHR. According to the case law of the ECtHR, Member States may not evade their obligation to protect Convention rights by joining an international organization and transferring to it the authority to undermine these very rights.[48] However, such concerns are unfounded with regard to Union law, as the fundamental rights of the ECHR are part of Union law as general principles pursuant to Art. 6 par. 3 of the TEU, even if the Union as such has not yet acceded to the ECHR, contrary to the mandate contained in Art. 6 par. 2 of the TEU. As far as the implementation and application of Union law is concerned, corporate freedom of religion is also contained in the primary law norm of Art. 10 par. 1 of the CFR.

Art. 9 par. 1 of the GDPR prohibits the processing of data revealing religious or philosophical beliefs. However, the prohibition does not apply if one of the exceptions listed in par. 2 is fulfilled.

If the data processing is carried out on the basis of suitable guarantees by a foundation, association or other non-profit organization with a political, philosophical, religious or trade union orientation[49] in the context of its legitimate activities, the prohibition of Art. 9 par. 1 of the GDPR pursuant to par. 2 lit. d does not apply if the processing relates exclusively to the members or former members of the organization or to persons who maintain regular contact with it in connection with its purpose of activity and the personal data are not disclosed externally without the consent of the data subjects.

This exemption provision reflects Art. 17 par. 1 of the TFEU, which obliges the Union to respect and not to prejudice the respective status enjoyed by churches and religious associations or communities in the Member States under their legislation. At the same time, the Regulation balances the autonomy of religious communities, which is protected by fundamental rights (Art. 10 par. 1 CFR, Art. 9 par. 1 ECHR), the protection of personal data under fundamental rights (Art. 8

47 Austria's obligation under international law remains unaffected by the primacy of Union law but would oblige the Republic to break the Concordat in the event of a genuine conflict.

48 *Aust*, A Union friendly to international law? Reasons for and limits to the opening of European law to international law, EuR 2017, 106–120 (117) with reference to ECtHR, judgment of 18.02.1999, *Waite & Kennedy v. Germany, appl. no. 26083/94.*

49 The internal data processing of the different categories of tendency organizations is protected. According to the wording, the criterion of no intention to make a profit is to be applied to all of the organizations mentioned but does not mean that the organization or a subdivision directly attributable to it is not allowed to generate the material basis for the realization of its tendency-based task. With further references, see *Kastelitz/Hötzendorfer/Tschohl* in: *Knyrim*, DatKomm, Art 9 GDPR, par. 39 (as of 7.5.2020, rdb.at).

CFR) and other individual freedoms such as the right to private and family life (Art. 7 CFR, Art. 8 par. 1 ECHR). Prerequisites for lawfulness are membership or continuation of a former membership or a relationship that essentially resembles membership because there is regular contact between the person and the religious organization. The processing must be carried out in the context of lawful activities, which easily applies to the profession of religion for religious organizations. The permissibility of data processing does not include the permissibility of disclosing the data to the outside world. Explicit consent is required for this.

The criteria are met if a hospital is run by a church or religious society and, moreover, is not operated with the primary intention of participating in commercial transactions, but as an expression and for the realization of its own self-image, which is protected by fundamental rights. However, in the interests of coherent protection of fundamental rights, the permissibility of disclosure to external persons involved in pastoral care in hospitals without consent only applies to pastoral care integrated into the church hospital. The admissibility also only applies to those patients who belong to the same religious community to which the hospital is affiliated.

For the large number of public and private hospitals, the question of whether they are obliged to pass on the data is not answered in Art. 9 par. 2 lit. d of the GDPR, as it is not the religious society but the institution that acts as the processor.

If a patient is dying, the application of Art. 9 par. 2 lit. c of the GDPR comes into consideration. If the patient is unable to give consent for physical or legal reasons and the processing is necessary to protect the vital interests of the data subject, it is lawful. Since neither the religiously and ideologically neutral state nor the organs of a hospital are entitled to decide whether, for example, the reception of the last rites is "vital", the processing of data for the purpose of passing it on to the religious community is not only lawful but also necessary in this extreme case of hospital pastoral care.

Finally, the application of the exception standardized in lit. g leg. cit. may also be considered: The processing of sensitive data is permitted if it has a legal basis in Union law or the law of the Member State. In this case, the processing must be proportionate to the objective pursued, respect the essence of the right to data protection and provide for appropriate and specific measures to safeguard the fundamental rights and interests of the data subject. Furthermore, the processing must be necessary for reasons of substantial public interest.

Art. 15 of the StGG and Sec. 18 of the ProtG form a legal basis in national (constitutional) law. Insofar as the information is given exclusively to the responsible chaplain, the proportionality to the pursued goal of carefully reconciling the rights of patients and religious communities is given. The essence of the fundamental right to data protection is safeguarded and appropriate and specific measures to protect the fundamental rights and interests of the data subject are in place insofar as the subsequent use and processing of the data by the religious community is only permitted within the narrow limits of lit. d. Violations of this are punishable by sanctions. The question of a significant public interest could be controversial. The answer to the question of whether such an interest exists must be found solely in the legal system. The receipt of information is a prerequisite for religious communities to be able to exercise a subjective right guaranteed by constitutional law. Without this knowledge, the "administration" of an internal matter of most religious societies would be considerably more difficult. Insofar as Art. XVI of the ÖK forms the legal basis for Catholic hospital chaplaincy, a considerable public interest can be seen in the Republic of Austria's adherence to the treaty. Finally, the application of Union law in conformity with fundamental rights constitutes a considerable public interest.[50] Should the question become virulent in judicial proceedings, the binding decision on the effect of Art. 10 of the CFR and Art. 17 of the TFEU on the application of this exception would be up to the ECJ in the context of a preliminary ruling procedure under Art. 267 of the TFEU.

The ECtHR first dealt with the question of the relationship between the corporate practice of religion and data protection in the case Jehovah's Witnesses v. Finland in 2023.[51] The ban on the collection and processing of personal data of non-members on the occasion of door-to-door visits by Jehovah's Witness missionaries does not violate Art. 9 of the ECHR. For several reasons, however, the case cannot be transferred to solve data protection issues in the context of hospital chaplaincy. The collection of protected data on the occasion of the door-to-door preaching of a religious doctrine involves data from strangers. In contrast, the issue of data protection in the context dealt with here revolves exclusively around data of persons who belong to the religious community voluntarily and whose membership is also recognized under state law. Therefore, the question of whether a patient must expressly consent to the disclosure of the data or whether the membership requested on the occasion of admission contains an implied consent is not comparable with the collection of data that takes place on the basis of randomly contacted persons at their home.

---

50 See also Recital 55: "The processing of personal data by public authorities for the purposes of the constitutional or international objectives of religious communities recognized by the State is also carried out for reasons of public interest."

51 Cf. ECtHR, 09.05.2023, *Jehovah's Wittnesses v. Finland*, appl. no.31172/19.

V. Summary

Like the Austrian Concordat, the religious recognition laws also regulate pastoral care of the sick primarily as a state facilitation of the exercise of an internal affair within the meaning of Art. 15 of the Basic Law. The individual legal perspective is only indirectly taken into account. In contrast, the Patients' Charter and hospital law address the issue of pastoral care from a perspective that focuses exclusively on the individual patient and their articulated wishes. This circumstance does not make it any easier to deal with the conflict of interests that already exists at the level of constitutionally protected subjective rights and leaves it up to the practitioner of the law to strike the constitutionally required balance.

The problem under data protection law is that the processing of the data is carried out by the hospitals and therefore the tendency-protecting exception of Art. 9 par. 2 lit. d of the GDPR is not applicable, unless it concerns pastoral care for patients of one's own religious society in a hospital under the sponsorship of this very religious society.

The processing of the data and its disclosure exclusively for the purpose of hospital chaplaincy can therefore only be based on Art. 9 par. 2 lit. g of the GDPR. However, the facts are so much in need of interpretation that a solution that is both compliant with EU law and Austrian constitutional law suggests that the issue of providing information to hospital chaplains should be explicitly standardized in the federal and provincial laws.

In view of the constitutional right of churches and religious societies, guaranteed in the individual recognition laws and in the 1933/34 Concordat, to fulfil their respective mission towards their own sick and dying members, the requirement of a wish must not be interpreted as an explicit positive expression of will. Membership of a recognized church or religious society continues to have an effect on state law as long as it is not terminated by a declaration of resignation to the state authorities. Membership gives rise to the binding presumption that, in the event of a case, pastoral care will be made use of as long as no contrary intention is expressed. This is particularly virulent in the case of patients who can no longer express their own wishes. If one were to aim for an explicit expression of consent and not attribute any explanatory value to formal religious affiliation, coma patients would lose the right to spiritual support in an extreme health situation.

As stated at the beginning, the individual right to religious freedom also has an effect on one's own community, so that the presumption of affiliation can be rebutted at any time. However, the requirement of explicit consent assumes from the outset that the member of a religious community has an internal reserve to their own religion. The solution already found in Sec. 20 par. 3 of the NÖ KAG,[52] that the patient can expressly object, takes this multipolar tension into account and offers itself as a model for a nationwide legal solution.

52 "Unless the patient expressly forbids it, the persons employed in the hospital may provide information on request in individual cases as to whether the patient has been admitted to the hospital and where they can be found. This also applies mutatis mutandis to religious care."

Spiritual Care to Austrian Armed Forces-Assessment of the Current Situation and Perspectives with Regard to Religious Law

HARALD TRIPP

I. Introduction

I.1 Church and religious society "in event"[1]

In many European countries, legal systems contain some special provisions with regard to the exercise of religious freedom by persons who are in public institutions that legally restrict everyday life and the normal habits associated with it due to special circumstances.[2] These include, in particular, the military, the police, prisons, hospitals and nursing homes.[3] These areas are therefore referred to as functional or categorical pastoral care, as they are forms of realisation of churches and religious communities that are not merely territorially organised or divided into territorially defined units.[4] Churches and religious communities are assigned here to a specific personal area of social life. They are therefore a group of believers who are not bound to a specific territory, but who have a certain similarity in their structures due to a specific function within public social life and who come together in regular religious assemblies. In them, however, the churches and religious communities really are in "event" (im Ereignis).[5]

---

1 The text of the presentation in Prague is based on an introductory lecture at the Seggau Talks between Church and State 2022. For the present paper, the text was shortened and updated. For the original version *Tripp,* Militärseelsorge-Standortbestimmung und Perspektiven im Blick auf das österreichische Religionsrecht, *Esterbauer/Grabenwarter/Pabel,* Kategoriale Seelsorge. Seggauer Gespräch zu Staat und Kirche 2022 (Band 2), Wien 2024, p. 1–16.

2 *Balodis/Blanco* (ed.), Religious assistance in public institutions, Proceedings of the XXVIIIth Annual Conference Jurmala, 13–16 October 2016, 2018, Granada, p. 3.

3 See explanations at *Greinacher,* Grundsätzliches zur funktionalen Gemeinde, in *Arnold/Rahner/Schurr/Weber/Klostermann* (ed.), Handbuch der Pastoraltheologie III, 1968, p. 263.

4 Church takes place wherever the Gospel happens. Local church thus becomes an open network of many places and opportunities. See the article by *Schüßler/Schweighofer* (ed.), Kirche als Netzwerk pastoraler Orte und Ereignisse. Empirische Erkundungen und theologische Perspektiven, 2022.

5 *Schüßler/Schweighofer,* (Note 4), p. 265.

I.2 Guaranteeing the practice of religion

Irrespective of the personal and social relevance of a person's religious attitude or practice, according to *Potz* "the guarantee of the exercise of religion [...] must also be given in circumstances that make it significantly more difficult for the individual to exercise fundamental rights."[6] *Richard Potz* argues that positive state measures can or even must therefore be provided for in particularly precarious areas or situations of life. So if the state supports the exercise of religious practice through organisational measures or financial means, it must not privilege or discriminate, but this does not detract from the strict institutional separation of state and church or religious society. In this context, the term "accepting or taking in neutrality" ("hereinnehmende Neutralität") is used: the religious neutrality of the state is demonstrated precisely by the fact that it does not marginalise religion.[7]

II. Fundamentals of religious law for military chaplaincy in Austria

II.1 General principles

In Article 9a (1) and (2) of the Federal Constitution, the Republic of Austria commits itself to "comprehensive national defence", which includes military, spiritual, civil and economic national defence.[8] Military defence is the responsibility of the federal army, which is to be "established in accordance with the principles of a militia system" (Art 79 Abs 1 B-VG).[9] "Every male Austrian citizen shall be liable to military service" (Art 9a Abs 3 S 1 B-VG).[10] Art 14 of the Basic Law of the State (StGG) of 21 December 1867 on the general rights of citizens (StGG) and also Art 9 Abs 2 European Convention on Human Rights of 4 November 1950 (ECHR) expressly guarantee everyone full freedom of faith and conscience.[11] The basis of pastoral care to military personal in Austria under international law is Article VIII of the Concordat between the Holy See and the Republic of Austria from 1933/34.

---

6 *Potz*, Recht auf seelsorgliche Betreuung aus der Sicht der Patienten und der Religionsgemeinschaften, in *Körtner/Müller/Kletecka-Pulcker/Inthorn* (ed.), Spiritualität, Religion und Kultur am Krankenbett, 2009, p. 115.

7 *Bielefeldt*, Die Religionsfreiheit – ein vielfach missverstandenes Menschenrecht, in *Karl* (ed.), Religionsfreiheit im Zeichen der Globalisierung und Multikulturalität, 2013, p. 25.

8 *Rees*, Die katholische Militärseelsorge in Österreich als kirchliche und staatliche Einrichtung, in *Wagnsonner/Trauner/Lapin* (ed.), Kirchen und Staat am Scheideweg? 1700 Jahre Mailänder Vereinbarung, 2015, p. 193. Siehe auch *Brünner*, Gewissensfreiheit und Militärdienst aus verfassungsrechtlicher Sicht, in *Kohlhofer* (ed.), Gewissensfreiheit und Militärdienst, 2000, p. 41–45.

9 *Muzak*, B-VG 6ed. (2020) Art 79 B-VG.

10 *Muzak*, B-VG 6ed. (2020) Art 79 B-VG.

11 *Rees*, Die katholische Militärseelsorge, p. 193.

Article 10 (1) of the Federal Constitution (B-VG) stipulates that the Republic of Austria has the legislative and executive powers to implement military chaplaincy ("Gesetzgebungs- und Vollzugskompetenz").

The military chaplaincy today – despite its long tradition – therefore has no connection with the state's desire for spiritual counselling of the military service, which is based on older ideas of state-church law. Rather, it arises from the need to ensure the religious freedom of the individual soldier under today's conditions.[12] In this sense, it is a joint affair of churches and religious communities and the state. This cooperation creates as *Richard Potz* states an "institutional duality",[13] but the matters can be separated according to competences. It can be said that military chaplaincy is an external matter as far as its state organisation is concerned, but an internal church matter as far as its content is concerned.

This institutional provision for the religious freedom of individual members of the military is justified

a) by consideration for the individual's freedom of faith and conscience Article 14 of the Basic Law ("Staatsgrundgesetz"), even under the conditions of the army, under a "special relationship of force", and
b) by the right of churches and religious societies under Article 15 of the Basic Law to practise their religion together in public ("Korporationsgarantie" – corporate guarantee).[14]

II.2 Catholic military chaplaincy

In Austria, Catholic military chaplaincy was reorganised in 1773 with the establishment of an Apostolic Field Vicariate, which was territorially reorganised in 1869. With the outbreak of the First World War, the changeover from peacetime chaplaincy to field chaplaincy began, and at the end of the war the Apostolic Field Vicariate was dissolved. After the creation of the professional army in 1920, an army provostry (Heerespropstei) was established, and in 1924 it was renamed to military vicariate.[15] After the Second World War and the conclusion of the State

---

12 *Seiler*, Seelsorge in Bundeswehr und Bundesgrenzschutz, in HdbStKR II², 1995, p. 961. See in detail *Scheuner*, Die rechtliche Stellung der Kirchen in der Entwicklung von Staat und Gesellschaft, Militärseelsorge, 1972, p. 237.

13 *Schwarz*, Militärseelsorge in Österreich. Ihre Stellung in Staat und Kirche, in *Trauner* (ed.), Militärseelsorge. Kirche und Staat, 2005, Wien, p. 17. Auch *Ermacora*, Soldat und Religionsfreiheit, in Pax et Iustitia. Festschrift für Alfred Kostelecky zum 70. Geburtstag, 1990, Berlin, p. 86–88.

14 *Schwarz* in *Trauner*, p. 17.

15 See in detail *Reichl-Ham*, Die Entwicklung der Militärseelsorge vor dem Ersten Weltkrieg, in *Freistetter/Dabringer* (ed.), Religionen im Krieg 1914–1918. Katholische Kirche in Österreich, 2014, 102 (114–116).

Treaty 1955, in 1956, military chaplaincy was re-established as a military vicariate.[16] After the Apostolic Constitution "Spirituali militum curae" (SMC) of 21 April 1986, a separate military ordinariate was established in Austria in 1989 with its own statutes.[17] Initially, following the instructions of the Apostolic Constitution, the existing military vicariate was renamed to Military Ordinariate of the Republic of Austria by decree of 1 April 1987.[18] It became effective under constitutional law on 15 April 1987 and it is also called Military diocese (Militärdiözese).

Full episcopal rights were with SMC transferred to the bishop of the respective state, putting the military ordinarius on an equal level with a diocesan bishop. The statutes of the military ordinariate also stipulate that "the ecclesiastical appointment of [...] military chaplains is made by the military ordinarius after prior agreement with the Federal Minister of Defence."[19] State appointments are made in accordance with state law, including social security, salary, health insurance and retirement salary in accordance with c. 281 § 1–3 CIC.[20]

The military chaplancies are established according to territorial principles at the military commands and at the schools and academies. There are currently 17 Catholic military parishes in Austria, divided into two deanery areas (East and West), as well as three more at the Austrian contingents abroad in Bosnia-Herzegovina, Kosovo and Lebanon. It is emphasised that the Federal Ministry of Defence (BMLV) and its subordinate offices provide "the personnel and material expenses required for Catholic military chaplaincy" and that "Catholic military chaplaincy and its organs [...] are subject only to the Military Bishop of Austria in spiritual and pastoral matters."[21] The Bishop "shall make more detailed provisions on the exercise of Catholic military chaplaincy [...] by his own decree."[22]

---

16 *Gradauer*, Die Anfänge der Heeres-Seelsorge in Österreich, in Pax et Iustitia. Festschrift für Alfred Kostelecky zum 70. Geburtstag, 1990, Berlin, p. 443; auch besonders *Kostelecky*, Militärordinariat der Republik Österreich, ÖAKR 1990, p. 125.

17 Regarding statutes see *Kongregation für die Bischöfe*, Dekret Nr 155/88 vom 21. März 1989, in Abl. ÖBK Nr 3, 15. April 1989, Nr 42, 45; published in: AfkKR 1989, 184; *Österreichische Bischofskonferenz*, Statuten des Militärordinariates der Republik Österreich vom 15. April 1989, in ABl ÖBK, Nr 3, 15. April 1989, Nr 42, 45–48; published in: AfkKR 1989, 186.

18 GZ 10.200/403-1.2/87.

19 See Statutes 4b).

20 *Wessely*, Die Militärdiözese – eine Grenzgängerin, SPRW 2012 VuV A, 79 (104).

21 *Bundesministerium für Landesverteidigung*, Katholische Militärseelsorge, Richtlinien – Neufassung September 2005. Erlass vom 30. September 2005, GZ S 90594/1-Zentr/2005, in VBl 2005 17. Oktober, Nr 84, samt 3 Beilagen: Fachdienstanweisung für den Dekanatspfarrer/katholisch, Fachdienstanweisung für den Militärpfarrer/katholisch; Fachdienstanweisung Pfarradjunkt/katholisch, A. 2.

22 Richtlinien A.3.

II.3 Protestant military chaplaincy

In view of the extensive reforms by the former K. u. K. Imperial Ministry of Defence in 1869, the Protestant military chaplains were no longer placed under the Apostolic Field Vicariate, but under a Protestant military superintendent.[23] The legal situation for the Protestant military chaplaincy was shaped after the establishment of the Protestant military chaplaincy on 1 February 1957, when on 6 July 1961, with the so-called "Protestants Act" ("Protestantengesetz") in § 17, the federal legislator also guaranteed and regulated pastoral care in the army for the Protestant Church in analogy to the Concordat provisions of 1933.[24] According to § 17 Abs 2 Protestants Act, the Protestant military chaplaincy is subordinate in spiritual matters to the Protestant Church A. B. and H. B., and in administrative and pension matters to the relevant command authorities. Seven Protestant military pastors are currently deployed in the Austrian Armed Forces under the leadership of a military superintendent.

II.4 Religious care – orthodox

The Orthodox Bishops' Conference, which represents all Orthodox churches recognised in Austria and all Orthodox Christians living in Austria, established the current Orthodox Military Chaplaincy on 1 July 2011. Apart from the provisions of the StGG 1867, reference could be made to the "Orthodox Act" (Orthodoxengesetz), which contains provisions on military chaplaincy from which a "legal entitlement to a separate Greek-Oriental military chaplaincy" could be mandatorily derived.[25] The Greek-Oriental Metropolis of Austria with its seat in Vienna, which according to Greek-Oriental law is directly subordinate to the Ecumenical Patriarchate, has the status of a corporation under public law (Körperschaft öffentlichen Rechts) as a state-recognised institution of the Greek-Oriental Church in Austria

---

23 The Protestant military superintendent at the international conference for military bishops in Vienna in July recently emphasised the significance of the 1781 Toleration Act (Toleranzpatent) issued by the Habsburgs. *Trauner*, Die staatkirchliche Situation in Österreich, pro manuscripto uncorrected concept by the author dated 16 June 2024, p. 1–2.

24 The Protestant Act 1961 refers to more detailed regulations in military law: Decrees of 29 March 1984 (Zl. 10200/621-1.2/84.III.B2–4b), 11 november 1987 (Verlautbarungsblatt I Nr 7/5 February 1988). This decree has since been replaced by decree of 13 April 2005, GZ S90595/4- Präs/2005, VBl I 45/2005. See in particular the summary in *Trauner*, Vom Gestern ins Morgen. Evangelische Militärseelsorge im Österreichischen Bundesheer, 2022, p. 62–64. Older, but more fundamental on this subject is Rechtsgrundlagen der Evangelischen Militärseelsorge. Die legitimen Forderungen der evangelischen Kirche Österreichs an den Staat und ihre geschichtliche Begründung, in *Trauner* (ed.), Militärseelsorge. Kirche und Staat, 2005, p. 8.

25 Decree by Ministry of Defense BMLVS S90597/4-Präs/2011 vom 4.8.2011, A.2 (not published).

in accordance with § 6 Orthodox Act.[26] It is therefore the sole and exclusive point of contact for the Austrian state with regard to all other Orthodox parishes and communities in accordance with the applicable legal system.

The chaplain appointed by the Orthodox Bishops' Conference is not a member of the Austrian Armed Forces (and also not on duty at the BMLV), does not wear a uniform and has only limited opportunities within the Armed Forces. The Orthodox military chaplain receives a special access pass from the BMLV, similar to the regulation with the Islamic and Alevi military chaplains, in order to have access to the military areas. Officially, religious counselling has not yet been regulated in the usual way of the official bulletin for reasons that are not yet clear.

II.5 Religious counselling – Islamic (IGGÖ-ALEVI)

With the enlistment of Bosnian recruits after the occupation of Bosnia-Herzegovina in 1881 and thus the existence of Islamic soldiers in the Austro-Hungarian army, special regulations were introduced for the protection of religious care. In 1882, special regulations were issued for the protection of the religious needs and customs of Bosnian conscripts.[27] In 1882, the appointment of separate field imams led to the establishment of an Islamic military chaplaincy and the construction of a separate military mosque. Due to the growing proportion of Muslims in the Austrian population, the question of an institutionalised Islamic military chaplaincy became topical again at the beginning of the 21st century. At present (2024), Islamic military chaplaincy is provided by two IGGÖ chaplains, one each for eastern and western Austria. In 2002, a prayer room was set up in the Maria Theresien Kaserne in Vienna, ceremonially opened in 2004 and converted into a mosque in 2006. 2024 was opened a prayer room in the Military Academy of Wiener Neustadt. In the Islam Act 2015, the Islamic Religious Community in Austria and the Alevi Religious Community in Austria (ALEVI) were granted the right to look after Muslims in the armed forces for the first time on a legal basis in Section 11 (1) and Section 18 (1).[28]

---

26 See the comments in my contribute *Tripp*, Militärseelsorge – Orthodox, in LKRR III, 2020, p. 251.
27 See for this *Ham*, Von den Anfängen der Militärseelsorge bis zur Liquidierung des Apostolischen Feldvikariates im Jahr 1918, in *Gröger/Ham/Sammer* (ed.), Zwischen Himmel und Erde. Militärseelsorge in Österreich, 2001, 13 (66–67). For the period of the First World War, see *Reichl-Ham*, Die religiöse Betreuung von muslimischen Soldaten im Ersten Weltkrieg, in *Trauner/Reichl-Ham* (ed.), Religionen im Krieg 1914–1918. Griechisch-orientalische (orthodoxe) Kirche, Islamitische Glaubensgemeinschaft, Israelitische Religionsgesellschaft in der Habsburgermonarchie, 2014, 287 (295–297).
28 See also Religious counselling for members of the armed forces who are members of the IGGiÖ; revised version of the guidelines 2015, BMLV decree of 15 July 2015, GZ S90598/5-Präs/2015, VBl I 43/2015; Religious counselling for members of the Armed Forces who are members of the Alevi

II.6 Religious counselling – Jewish

Initially, there was no provision for pastoral care for Jewish soldiers, who were only admitted to military service under Emperor Joseph II. in 1788. The need for pastoral care for the increasing number of Jewish soldiers in the Austro-Hungarian army was discussed intensively in 1866 and Rabbi Alexander Kisch (1848–1917) was appointed the first field rabbi of the reserve in 1874.[29] The care of Jewish soldiers in peacetime was provided by local civilian rabbis. At present, the religious counselling of Jewish soldiers is carried out on behalf of the Jewish law 2012.[30]

Regarding religious minorities in general there exist some special regulations.[31] In 2003, all special regulations (leave of absence, dining regulations, clothing) were summarised and published in a single decree (BMLV, VBl. I, No. 49/2003). This was revised in 2006 (BMLV, VBl. I, No. 53/2006). It regulates the special provisions for soldiers who belong to one of the following five religious organisations (Altk. Church, Evangelical Church A.B./H.B, Evangelical Methodist Church, Islamic Religious Community in Austria, the Israelite Religious Society) or two denominations (Seventh-day Adventist Church and the Sikh denomination). Adapted again in 2018 (Decree of 31/08/2018, GZ S93109/4- MFW/2018, VBl. I 92/2018), corresponding regulations are made here with regard to the conscription, treatment and use of conscripts and persons performing training service who are strictly religious members (strenggläubig) of legally recognised churches and religious comunities, e.g.: Training, uniforms, time regulations, public holidays and catering.

Religious Community (ALEVI); 2016 version of the guidelines, BMLV decree of 31 Aug. 2016, GZ S90596/7-Präs/2016, VBl I 54/2016. See also § 11 Abs 3, 18 Abs. 3 IslamG.

29 *Ham* in *Gröger/Ham/Sammer*, p. 62–64.

30 Religious counselling for members of the armed forces who are members of the Israelite Religious Religious Society (IRG), BMLV decree of 7 Feb. 2018, GZ S90596/2-Präs/2018, VBl I 37/2018, based on § 8 Abs 1 IsraelitenG.

31 *Tripp*, Militärseelsorge, in *Kowatsch/Pichler/Tibi/Tripp* (ed.), *111 Begriffe des österreichischen Religionsrechts*, 2022, St. Ottilien, p. 227–232.

III. Military chaplaincy – tasks in a special field of categorical pastoral care of Churches and religious communities

III.1 A present dialogue partner

The tasks of military chaplaincy are manifold.[32] Military chaplains are present dialogue partners who are not direct superiors, but who nevertheless know the military system. If problems are raised with them, there is no need to first explain the wider environment. Indeed, even the people involved hardly need to be introduced, because the military chaplain lives in the military compounts, eats in the same dining hall and knows the soldiers at every level. Various forms and rituals of religious services, devotions, celebrations and speeches on various occasions are offered and organised by the military chaplaincy.

III.2 The training areas of ethics and religious studies

A specific point of attack of many a criticism of the military chaplaincy is the location of the life skills lessons (Lebenskundlicher Unterricht, LKU). It is provided by military chaplains as part of military training.[33] Although it is based on the foundations of the respective religious doctrine and content, it is not regarded as a matter for the respective church and religious community and does not enjoy the guarantee of spiritual autonomy. The fact that chaplains are called upon to provide this immaterial life support by the state is a matter for the state to decide freely. It could also call upon army psychologists for this purpose. According to *Karl Schwarz*, the commissioning of military chaplains appears to be "unobjectionable under constitutional law".[34]

The preparation of future instructors and commanders in particular is also about imparting ethical education in the sense of military ethics and political ethics beyond purely legal training, developing sufficient self-confidence to critically analyse circumstances, make appropriate judgements and decisively do what is recognised as right. The prudent commander is characterised by the respectful

---

32 The wide range is summarised in *Gugerel*, Feldspiritualität? Katholizismus und Militär aus der Perspektive eines Militärseelsorgers, Factum 2 WS 16/17, Magazin der Austro-Danubia zu Linz, 10. See further *Tripp*, Die Diözesansynode 2013 des Militärordinariates der Republik Österreich. Anmerkungen zur kanonistischen Praxis im pastoralen Prozess einer Teilkirche, in *Rees* (ed.), Synodale Prozesse in der katholischen Kirche, 2016, p. 335.

33 *Katholische Militärseelsorge*, Richtlinien – Neufassung September 2005, BMLV Erl v. 30. September 2005, GZ S 90594/1-Zentr/2005, VBl 84 vom 17. Okt. 2005, C. I. See also guidelines Final document of the diocesan synod, n. 17.

34 *Schwarz* in *Trauner*, p. 17.

treatment of his own soldiers and the intelligent use of their specific qualities, not least the language and cultural competence of Austrian soldiers with a migration background.

III.3 Military chaplaincy in peace keeping missions

In peace keeping deployments (currently Bosnia-Herzegovina, Kosovo, Lebanon and Mali), chaplains can express the supranational dimension of religion even more clearly by bringing together members of different nations at church services.[35] In addition, contact with religious representatives on the ground can create a climate of trust and solidarity that is useful and valuable for the deployment as a whole. The military chaplain is not a secret agent who spies on the population of the theatre of operations nor an ambassador for an international force. He makes it clear, beyond all problems and language barriers, that religiosity – regardless of the religion in which it is realised – is something unifyingly human.[36]

III.4 A cooperation partner in the Austrian Armed Forces

Cooperation, especially with those responsible for training cadre personnel in the fields of law and political education, enables the military chaplain to broaden and develop his own perspective and views.[37] The interdisciplinary dialogue with graduates of various military science subjects and above all the close cooperation with military medicine and military psychology open up theology and enrich the other sciences as well as social facilities, institutions and federal ministries.

III.5 Ecumenical and interreligious cooperation

Ecumenical and interreligious cooperation is a matter of course within the Austrian Armed Forces.[38] Christian, Jewish, Muslim and also non-believing soldiers can work together on joint projects and missions without any complications, regardless of their denomination. The same applies to the representatives of the official military chaplaincies of individual religious communities.

---

35 *Katholische Militärseelsorge,* Concept for peace keeping missions (not published).
36 Guidelines Final document of the diocesan synod, n. 23.
37 Guidelines Final document of the diocesan synod, nr. 29–32.
38 Guidelines Final document of the diocesan synod, nr. 22.

IV. Concluding perspectives and Challenges – are we getting more secular in Austria?

In public institutions, the law serves to maintain order between the political community and the recognised churches and religious societies are always realised like initially said "in event".

IV.1 Safeguarding the practice of religion

Pastoral care in the Austrian Armed Forces is intended to ensure the exercise of religion even under circumstances that would otherwise make it impossible or significantly more difficult for the individual to exercise this fundamental right.[39]

It is therefore also to be seen in the sense of a material understanding of fundamental rights under the aspect of "state duties to protect" ("staatliche Schutzpflichten"). Freedom of religion is thus enshrined and guaranteed by state law in these special areas of civil life.

IV.2 Military chaplaincy versus religious counselling

a) Outsourcing of pastoral care versus integration – where are we heading?

The Catholic and Protestant military chaplaincies were "institutionalised" with the re-establishment of the Austrian Armed Forces. Section 8 of the Service Ranks Ordinance 2018 (Dienstgradeverordnung) lists the respective military service ranks and pay grades for Catholic and Protestant chaplains in the Austrian Armed Forces.[40] Orthodox, Muslim, Islamic-Alevi and Jewish chaplains, on the other hand, are not part of the Austrian Armed Forces in the sense of an employment relationship and are remunerated at a very low level for their pastoral care. It has already been noted that this is probably a violation of the equal treatment of other religious communities in the sense of parity according to Art 15 Basic Law of 1867.[41] It can be assumed that outsourcing, especially in the area of churches and religious communities, is very much in line with the idea of an increasingly secular

---

39 On the protection of fundamental rights, *Lienbacher*, § 12 Religiöse Rechte, in *Merten/Papier* (ed.), Handbuch der Grundrechte in Deutschland und Europa VII/1 (Grundrechte in Österreich), 2014, 445 (461).
40 Regulation of the Federal Minister of Defence on the use of military ranks (Dienstgradeverordnung 2018 – DGV 2018), in BGBl II Nr 135/2018.
41 *Trauner*, Wandel von Staat und Kirche am Fallbeispiel Militärseelsorge, öarr 2012, 174 (191).

state. The implementation that the Ministry of Defence is apparently aiming for in the Orthodox military chaplaincy is the far-reaching detachment from the traditional *res mixtae*.

However, the experiences of recent years also show the importance of being integrated into the organism of the Austrian Armed Forces for the Orthodox, Muslim and Jewish military chaplaincies, because integration is the basis of acceptance, which is absolutely necessary for pastoral work.

b) Challenges for military chaplaincy due to the GDPR 2018

The entry into force of the "General Data Protection Regulation" ("Datenschutzgrundverordnung" – GDPR) in 2018, which is directly applicable in all member states, finally created a standardised level of data protection in the European Union. From 2018, the BMLV will process the religious confession data of conscripts and persons eligible for military service on the basis of § 55a (1) (1) of the Military Service Act ("Wehrgesetz") 2001 (VVG 2001).[42] The prerequisite for this is that the person concerned gives their express consent to the processing.[43]

This means that the processing of religious beliefs is now only permitted if the data subject has also expressly consented to the processing voluntarily. The conditions for such consent are set out in Art. 8 GDPR. However, since the religious affiliation (e. g. Roman Catholic) does not necessarily result, it is not possible to consistently process the religious confession on the basis of this standard.

The collection of religious confession from conscripts and persons who are eligible for military service must always be carried out as part of the recruitment or aptitude test by means of a voluntary declaration of consent. However, it is essential to point out again during the recruitment or aptitude test that the disclosure and authorisation for the processing of religious confession provided for in the declaration of consent is voluntary and that conscripts are under no circumstances obliged to submit the declaration of consent.

This regulation initially creates a number of problem areas for the full-time military chaplaincy with regard to the voluntary disclosure of religious confession, as there is no verification in the sense of a survey by the BMLV itself, as well as the possibility of an individual change at any time. For the work of categorical pastoral care in public institutions, there is a problem area with regard to the nature of

---

42 Ss source an internal, unpublished document: *Federal Ministry of Defence*, Personnel matters – General; processing of religious confession, Decree (Erlass) of 13 August 2018, GZ S91354/25-PersA/2018 (1).

43 *Federal Ministry of Defence*, VBl 1 Directive for Data Protection in the Federal Ministry of Defence, decree of 17 December 2018, GZ S90181/10-Präs/2018, point 5.1.

standardisation, as it is not actually the survey itself, but the type of consent with regard to recording and processing, including forwarding to the military chaplaincy, that could be a hindrance or disadvantage for recording the actual number of persons requiring religious care with regard to pastoral care "in event".

V. Concluding Remarks

Not everyone is familiar with military chaplaincy and some may ask themselves: "Religion and the military: can they even go together?" Yet military chaplaincy is one of the oldest categorical forms of pastoral care. Because of their special living conditions, soldiers also need a specific and appropriate form of pastoral care. The military chaplains of all Churches and religious communities should always bear in mind that they may have to refuse an order or even leave the armed forces for reasons of conscience. Their credibility will then be judged by whether they are more committed to their conscience than to the pursuit of a secure income, social acceptance and relative security. In any case, the Austrian Armed Forces offer a tense space in which to realise one's Faith and pastoral care.

Spiritual Care in Public Institutions in Italy

STEFAN MÜCKL

I. Introduction

The concept of "spiritual assistance", "religious assistance" or "spiritual care" refers to the activity aimed at satisfying the religious needs of those citizens who are, temporarily or permanently, placed within obligatory structures ("*comunità chiuse*", "closed communities", such as prisons, hospitals, military forces). The fundamental idea of spiritual care is to mitigate the challenges associated with exercising religious freedom within the aforementioned institutions. It seeks to supplement the individual legal position of these citizens by granting religious communities access to these institutions.

Unlike other constitutions – such as the German constitution – the Italian constitution does not directly guarantee the institution of spiritual care in public institutions. Nevertheless, it has constitutional status, by way of the clause provided for in the constitution itself, which obliges the State authority to effectively guarantee fundamental rights. The substantial fundamental right is that of religious freedom – guaranteed in art. 19 –, and the reinforcing norm is art. 3 para. 2 of the Constitution:

> It is the duty of the Republic to remove those obstacles of an economic or social nature which constrain the freedom and equality of citizens, thereby impeding the full development of the human person and the effective participation of all workers in the political, economic and social organisation of the country.

Italian constitutional law does not contain any further specifications, neither about its more detailed organisation nor questions of its financing by the State. The legislator therefore has a wide margin of appreciation and discretion, which can only be limited by the standards determined by the general principle of equality.[1]

Further details can be found in the law currently applicable and in the contractual regulations agreed between the State and religious communities. For the

1 Art. 3 para. 1 of the Constitution: "All citizens have equal social dignity and are equal before the law, without distinction of [...] religion [...]".

Catholic Church, these are the Lateran pacts, which are incorporated into the Constitution in accordance with art. 7 para. 2. For the other religious communities, art. 8 para. 2 of the Constitution opens the possibility of concluding agreements (‘*intese*’) concerning their relations with the State. In both cases, these contractual regulations are legally binding and are passed by Parliament as laws (the only difference is that the conventions with the Catholic Church, if they are concluded with the Holy See, are international treaties – ‘concordats’ –, whereas the agreements with the minority confessions are of a purely domestic nature).

The current contractual framework in Italy is as follows: The Treaty of Villa Madama of 18 February 1984, which replaced the Concordat of 1929 – which was part of the Lateran pacts – applies to the Catholic Church.[2] It is generally accepted that this treaty also falls within in the constitutional guarantee of art. 7 para. 2. The State has concluded a total of 13 agreements with the minority confessions since 1984, starting with the Waldensian Evangelical Church (‘*Tavola valdese*’) and most recently – in 2019 – with the Association of the Church of England. Contractual partners are both Christian denominations (Lutherans, Orthodox, Baptists and other Protestant denominations) and non-Christian religions (Jews, Hindus and Buddhists). Up to now, however, there are no contractual relationships with Muslims[3] or Jehovah's Witnesses (although an agreement was signed in 2000, it was never approved by Parliament).

All of these treaties contain provisions relating to spiritual care in public institutions. Historically, it is worth noting that regarding the Catholic Church, this issue was already regulated in the Concordat in 1929. As is known, the Catholic Church was the State religion at that time. Nevertheless, other religious communities – insofar as they were recognised by the State – were not without protection: a royal decree of 28 February 1930 contained corresponding guarantees in hospitals and prisons as well as (in the case of mobilisation) in the armed forces.

II. General framework

In general, the principal lines of spiritual care in general can be summarised in these points:

- spiritual care is assumed to be necessary if there are members of a religious confession in an institution (who have not expressly refused spiritual care),

---

2 *Giovannelli*, The 1984 covenant between the Republic of Italy and the Vatican: A retrospective analysis after fifteen years, Journal of Church and State, 42.3, Summer 2000, pp. 529 ff.

3 *Morucci*, I rapporti con l'Islam italiano: dalle proposte d'intesa al Patto nazionale, Stato, Chiese e pluralismo confessionale, Rivista telematica, n. 38/2018.

- therefore, the ministers of a religious community have a right of access to the institution, which does not depend on the goodwill of management (in other words, the granting of access is not based on a discretionary power),
- in substance, spiritual care includes the exercise of religious practices and spiritual assistance,
- the State has a general duty of cooperation, which obliges it to create the necessary organisational conditions for religious activity in its institutions (*vice versa*, it prohibits it from being hindered). This duty is concretized by agreements.

Neither the nature nor the concept of spiritual care gives rise to a further State obligation, especially regarding financing. Different approaches and solutions can be found in this area, both in unilateral State legislation and in agreements, not a few times with surprising or differentiated content.

In France, for example – the prototype of the model of separation of Church and State – the *Law on the Separation of Church and State* (1905) provides that the State can assume the costs of institutional chaplaincy in public institutions and explicitly mentions schools, colleges, hospitals, asylums, and prisons. In Italy, on the other hand, a State that constitutionally co-operates with the Catholic Church and all other religious communities, we find a split system: In the case of the Catholic Church, the State bears the costs. On the other hand, minority confessions have to bear their own expenses, to which they have consented in the respective agreements with the State.

III. Spiritual care in the armed forces

III.1 Catholic Church

Historically, the oldest case of an institutional chaplaincy is a military chaplaincy, especially in the context of the Catholic Church. Since the beginning of the 20th century, the Holy See has established a hierarchical structure known as the military vicariate in various States, accordance with canon law. This military vicariate is largely independent of the general territorial structure of the Church, but at the same time serves to complete it. The Holy See subsequently sought (and usually obtained) additional contractual protection for this structure through concordats and agreements with the States. In a further step, the States then issued their own regulations for military chaplaincies, taking the position of the Church into account. Military chaplaincy thus proves to be a prime example of the so-called '*res mixtae*', in which Church and State co-operate both establishing the legal framework and in practice.

As is well known, it was only after the Second World War that the Holy See created a general framework for the military vicariates,[4] which was subsequently revised in 1986 by Pope John Paul II in accordance with the guidelines of the Second Vatican Council[5] and brought into its current form in the Apostolic Constitution *Spirtuali militum curae.*[6]

The Holy See first established a military vicariate for Italy in March 1926, which was recognised a year later by the law of the Italian State.[7] The Concordat of 1929 confirmed this legal framework.[8] Even after the Second World War and the transition from the monarchy to the republic, the military vicariate remained in existence, with the 1926 law repeatedly adapted to meet changing needs.[9] In 2010, this law was incorporated into the new Code of Military law ("*Codice dell'ordinamento militare*")[10]. In 1987, the Holy See issued new statutes for what is now known as the *military ordinariate.*[11] Through an exchange of notes in 2018,[12] approved by Parliament in 2021,[13] the Holy See and the Italian State set out the legal framework of the military chaplaincy now in force.

The Catholic military ordinariate in Italy is a jurisdictional structure of a personal nature. Its ministers are appointed by the competent ecclesiastical authority (as provided for in art. 11, para. 2 of the Treaty of Villa Madama). However, they are also integrated into the military structure and hold military ranks: the military bishop, who holds the personal rank of archbishop, is appointed by the Pope but formally nominated by the President of the Republic, with the rank of an army corps general. Other ministers hold lower officer ranks according to their positions. As a result of this integration into the military structure, the State bears the associated costs.

---

4 *Sacred Consistorial Congregation,* Instruction *Solemne semper,* 23 April 1953, Actae Apostolicae Sedis 43 (1951), pp. 562–565.

5 *Second Vatican Council,* Decree concerning the Pastoral Office of Bishops in the Church *Christus Dominus,* 28 October 1965, n. 43.

6 *John Paul II,* Apostolic Constitution *Spirituali militum curae,* 21 April 1986, Acta Apostolicae Sedis 78 (1986), pp. 481–486; c. 569 CIC refers to "special laws" (as did c. 451 § 3 CIC/1917: "peculiaribus Sanctae Sedis praescriptis").

7 *Legge 11 marzo* 1926, n. 417.

8 Art. 3.

9 *Legge 9 novembre 1955,* n. 1118; *Legge 1° giugno 1962,* n. 512.

10 *Decreto legislativo 15 marzo 2010,* n. 66; modified 2012.

11 *Statuto dell'Ordinariato militare per l'Italia,* 6 August 1987.

12 Epistularum permutatio inter Sanctam Sedem et Rempublicam Italicam de spirituali Militum cura, ad applicandum articulum 11 Pactionis recognitae Concordati Lateranensis, die 18 mensis Februarii 1984, Acta Apostolicae Sedis 113 (2021), pp. 1039–1053 = Acta Apostolicae Sedis 113 Numerus specialis (2021), pp. 98–112.

13 *Legge 22 aprile 2021,* n. 70. – See *Cavana,* La legge n. 70 del 2021 di riforma dell'assistenza spirituale ai cattolici nelle Forze armate e norme di adeguamento ad obbligazioni internazionali contratte con la Santa Sede. Osservazioni sulla crisi del principio di bilateralità nella XVIII Legislatura, Quaderni di diritto e politica ecclesiastico 30, 2022, pp. 469–489.

III.2 Minority confessions

The key difference between the regime of the Catholic Church and that of minority confessions does[14] not primarily lie in the legal position of the soldiers concerned – it is a question of guaranteeing their religious freedom as effectively as possible under the circumstances of military service. Instead, the distinction lies in the fundamental organisation of spiritual care. This is clearly illustrated by the Agreement with the Waldensian Evangelical Church (similar to the Treaty of Villa Madama from 1984). The stipulations made therein (art. 5) can also be found, with minor differences, in the agreements concluded later with other minority confessions. In detail:

- military personnel have the right to participate in the religious and ecclesiastical activities scheduled on specific days and times in the localities where they reside by reason of their military service,
- if no activities of worship are to take place in those localities, authorised ministers may conduct worship meetings in nearby places, previously agreed with the command on which the military personnel depend,
- in the case of the death of military personnel while on duty, the competent military command shall take the necessary measures to ensure that the funeral takes place according to the individual's respective liturgy,
- if a pastor of a confession is doing his military service, he shall be allowed to perform, together with their service obligations, spiritual care to the military personnel who request it,
- the financial burdens for the performance of any form of spiritual care shall be borne by the competent religious bodies.

As far as can be seen, to date, these provisions have proven to be sufficient for members of minority confessions. It should be added that – as in many other European countries – there is currently no compulsory military service (it was suspended with effect starting from 1 January 2005).

IV. Penal institutions

The objective of making available spiritual care in penal institutions is obviously to enable inmates to exercise their religious freedom. Historically, and perhaps also currently, a subcutaneous motivation still resonates, namely that of using spiritual

---

14 See *De Oto*, Il servizio di assistenza spirituale ai militari. Tra diritto confessionale e diritto dello Stato, 2020, Bologna.

assistance as a means to encourage inmates to repent and change their ways and thus facilitate their reintegration into society through moral education.

The current legal situation in Italy[15] has, once again, two levels: In the Treaty of Villa Madama and in the agreements with minority confessions, the State has undertaken to guarantee religious freedom in penal institutions and to ensure that inmates are cared for by the respective religious ministers.

The details of these rather general provisions can be found in a law on the penitentiary system from 1975,[16] which predates all of the current contractual agreements (and dates back to a time when Catholicism was still the State religion in Italy). This explains why a dual system also applies here: all inmates have the right to profess their faith, to be instructed in it and to practise their respective cult. The celebration of Catholic worship is guaranteed in the institutions, and there must be at least one chaplain in each institution. For the other religious communities, the law provides for a needs-based regulation: at their request, believers of other communities have the right to receive assistance from their religious ministers and to celebrate religious services.

In brief: ministers from non-Catholic communities have a right of access to penal institutions (as specified in the agreements, the communities inform the authorities of the ministers they have appointed and authorized). A real chaplaincy has been set up only for the Catholic Church; chaplains have an employment and disciplinary relationship with prison authorities and are paid by them. The details can be found in another law from 1982 (i. e. also enacted before the Treaty of Villa Madama).[17]

As in other European countries, an interesting development can be observed over the last ten years: in practice, it continues to be difficult to conclude agreements with Islamic communities, especially because their representativeness for Muslim believers is often not proven. One exception to this reluctance is precisely the penal system. For sociological reasons, there is a need for pragmatic arrangements with Muslim communities in penal institutions and in November 2015 the Italian Ministry of Justice concluded an administrative agreement with the Union of Islamic Communities and Organisations in Italy (UCOII). However, it essentially consists of the exchange of information: the judicial authorities provide the Islamic associations with a list of penal institutions with a significant proportion of Muslim inmates. For their part, the Islamic organisations provide lists of suitable ministers and volunteers for spiritual care.

In concluding this section, it is useful to briefly examine a specific legal problem in Italy concerning the penal system in a wider sense. Under certain conditions,

---

15 See *Santoro,* Religione e detenzione. La libertà religiosa oltre le mura carcerarie, 2020, Napoli.

16 *Legge 26 luglio 1975,* n. 354.

17 *Legge 4 marzo 1982,* n. 68.

shorter prison sentences (up to four years) can be served in house arrest instead of in prisons. For 40 years, it has been perceived as a legal problem the issue of how convicts can exercise their religious freedom in this case. Specifically, the question arises as to whether they are allowed to leave their homes to attend religious services. The Italian Code of Criminal Procedure stipulates as a rule that a convicted person may not leave their home. Exceptions due to "indispensable necessities of life" require a judge's order.[18] Whether attending a church service is such a "necessity" is highly controversial among the courts. In the 1980s some administrative courts answered the question in the affirmative, while others answered it in the negative. In 2012, the Court of Cassation followed a restrictive line and based its decision on the possibility of watching radio and television broadcasts of religious services (just like patients who are unable to move).[19] The line taken by the Catholic bishops in the 2020–2022 coronavirus pandemic is unlikely to make a future revision of this case law any easier. Apart from that, this is a matter where legislative intervention would certainly be helpful.[20]

V. Hospitals

As in other areas, there is a dual system in spiritual care in hospitals in Italy:[21] the Catholic Church has established a comprehensive system of institutional chaplaincies, with priests and other staff dedicated solely to this activity. For reasons of human resources, however, increasingly, a certain concentration can be observed (e.g. one priest being responsible for several hospitals), as well as an increased reliance on volunteers.

For the minority confessions, this is a case where the model of the right of free access also applies, in order to provide spiritual assistance to the faithful who so wish. This right has been in force since the aforementioned royal decree of 1930 and was extended in two stages after the Second World War. A law from 1968 with a subsequent decree from 1969 obliged the management of public hospitals to pass on the wishes of patients for spiritual assistance to the respective religious communities. A further law from 1978 stipulated that agreements were to be made with the religious communities, both with the Catholic diocesan bishops and with the other religious authorities in the catchment area of a hospital. Given this background,

---

18 Art. 284, para. 3 Code of Criminal Procedure.

19 Court of Cassation, IV Penal Section, 10 August 2012, n. 32364.

20 *Vitali/Chizzoniti*, Breve manuale Diritto Ecclesiastico, 2019, Milan, p. 221.

21 *Salido López*, Configuración jurídica de la asistencia religiosa en hospitales en Alemania, Italia y Portugal, Anuario del Derecho eclesiástico del Estado 39, 2023, pp. 49–79.

the agreements with the minority confessions since the 1980s have brought little that is new in the matter but have instead confirmed an ongoing practice.

In the meantime, a further differentiation can be seen in the area of spiritual care in hospitals. Now, the healthcare system is the competence of the Italian regions. The current legal situation allows them to conclude agreements on hospital chaplaincies with religious communities at a regional or local level. This has been done almost everywhere for the Catholic Church (partnering with the regional bishops' conferences), and occasionally also for non-Catholic confessions (at a regional level in Lombardy with the Jewish community, at the local level in Tuscany with the Jewish and Muslim communities). In substance, these agreements are dealing with means of facilitating the access of religious ministers to patients, providing suitable premises and, in some cases, ensuring compliance with religious dietary regulations.

The crucial point is, and remains, the safeguarding of religious freedom, especially in the face of the existential challenges of illness, suffering and imminent death. Accompanying the sick and dying and offering assistance during the transition from this world to the next, is a core aspect of pastoral care. This theory is hardly disputed, but, in practice, what a legal guarantee is worth is revealed only by an actual emergency. And precisely in such case, to a large extent, the guarantee was simply ignored during the corona pandemic (and not just in its first phase in March 2020). This should be the occasion for an honest and critical review.

Changes in Spiritual Care in the Czech Republic since 2019

ZÁBOJ HORÁK

In my article, I would like to focus on changes in spiritual care in the Czech Republic since 2019, when at our meeting I gave a report on the situation until that year and published it in the book *Tretera/Horák*, Spiritual Care in Public Institutions in Europe.[1]

The past period could be characterised by moderate and steady progress in spiritual care in public institutions. Above all, it was about the development of practice. Hard-working lawyers were responsible for the changes in practice and its contractual provision, such as Prof. Damián Němec from the Cyril and Methodius Faculty of Theology of Palacký University in Olomouc, who is personally involved in legislative preparations in the field of spiritual care in healthcare and Dr Adam Csukás, the chief lawyer of the Evangelical Church of Czech Brethren, in many fields.

I. A concordat agreement

Nevertheless, perhaps better times are close at hand in the area of spiritual care. Why is that? Because a concordat between the Apostolic See and the Czech Republic has already been prepared. It was signed in Prague on 24 October 2024. It was signed on behalf of the Holy See by His Eminence Cardinal Pietro Parolin, Secretary of State to His Holiness. His Excellence Petr Fiala, Prime Minister of the Czech Republic, signed it on behalf of the Czech Republic. If it is subsequently ratified on the recommendation of both chambers of the Parliament of the Czech Republic, the Concordat will fulfil the meaning of a special human rights convention and so will have greater legal force than the "ordinary" laws of the Czech Republic. This international convention contains provisions on spiritual care in various areas.

---

1 *Horák*, Spiritual Care in Public Institutions in the Czech Republic, in: *Tretera/Horák (eds.)*, Spiritual Care in Public Institutions in Europe, 2019, Berlin, p. 119–140.

The concordat would improve the standing of subjects of the Catholic Church. But in view of the system of parity between religious communities that is recognised in this country by both churches and secular authorities, other churches and religious communities would also acquire similar rights. This is the reason why not only the Catholic Church, but also other numerically important churches in the Czech Republic[2] expressed their decisive support for the Czech Concordat.

II. The root of our problems: the communist past

Let me digress slightly. Nine months ago I inherited the ancient seat of my ancestors 50 km north of Prague, in the small town of Mšeno in the middle of the Kokořínsko protected landscape area. I spent my childhood there and now I have partly moved back there. Father Jiří Rajmund Tretera OP, Professor of legal history and church law at the same faculty as me, has taken over the spiritual care of the eight churches and four chapels in the parish, which is almost as large as half the political district. I help him with this spiritual care as an altar server and driver.

What has this got to do with religion law? Well, I have a little more time to think and see various things from a different perspective than that of Prague. It's just that things are more visible in the countryside, they are not as obscured as in an intellectual, urban environment and, especially, the Prague environment.

I think that a lot of our problems, including problems with spiritual care in public institutions, have their roots in our communist past, which is only a few decades removed. So far, a large part of the Czech public has not been able to analyse or reject this past. Not only with words, but also with its civic attitude. Many people have not yet managed to recover from the atheism advocated by the communist state, nor from what continues to operate.

The communist way of thinking is even rooted in the church, especially among the laity.

III. A good starting position: the history of the Czech lands before the communist coup

And when it comes to spiritual care in public institutions? Spiritual care in the armed forces and in medical institutions has a tradition in the Czech lands dating back to the Middle Ages and spiritual care in prisons was built up, as in other parts

---

2 As for the numerical ratio between Catholics and members of other churches and religions in the Czech Republic, we can express it in values of approximately 80 to 20.

of the western part of the Austrian Empire (Cisleithania), to a comparable level. This arrangement was also adopted by the independent Czechoslovakia, which was established in 1918.

During the time of Nazism, all the churches in this country proved to be places of spiritual and practical resistance against the Nazi occupiers. In addition, Catholic parish priests in particular often helped Jews by issuing them with false baptism certificates to save them from dying in liquidation camps. Approximately 10 percent of Czech Catholic priests were persecuted by the Nazis for participating in the resistance movement.

The Orthodox Church was even banned by the Nazis and its leaders executed. The reason for this was that its members had provided their church as a hiding place for Czechoslovak parachutists sent from Great Britain, who carried out the successful assassination of the acting Reich Protector Reinhard Heydrich in Prague in May 1942.[3]

Catholic priests and the clergy of other churches were imprisoned together in Nazi prisons and concentration camps. *The first school of ecumenism.*

IV. A tragedy with terrible consequences: The 1948 communist putsch

The three post-war years of freedom were crushed by the communist putsch on 25 February 1948. All spheres of public life had to accept the so-called "scientific world view", the Marxist-Leninist ideology. This included atheism, which played the role of the state religion permanently and unchanged throughout the period between 1949–1989. Religious communities became the only alternatively thinking institutions whose existence was tolerated, but only to a small and limited extent. In order to perform the activities of a priest or preacher, it was necessary to obtain state approval, which could be withdrawn at any time and without justification.

State approval was often lost to priests who showed too much religious activity, especially when working with the younger generation, and who disobeyed the orders of hundreds of state officials authorized to supervise the churches in every town and the last village. Orders that aimed at the church to suppress its religious activity.

The sword of Damocles threatened any priest in the spiritual administration with the withdrawal of state approval until November 1989.

3 *Horák,* Geschichte und Gegenwart der Seelsorge in öffentlichen Einrichtungen in den böhmischen Ländern, in: Österreichisches Archiv für Recht und Religion, 2022/1, p. 113–114.

Part of the liquidation of a significant part of the clergy was the complete liquidation of all male orders in April 1950, the imprisonment of all religious in concentration camps and the impossibility of continuing the activities of religious orders until the beginning of 1990.

After the great rise of the Church after 1945, when the Czech theological faculties, diocesan and religious seminaries were as full as never before in the Czechoslovak Republic, the Catholic Church lost almost half of all its priests working in spiritual administration since 1949 (half of them were all religious priests, who were excluded from church work, and only after 15 to 20 years some of them returned to spiritual administration). All diocesan and religious seminaries were liquidated in 1949, the theological faculty in Olomouc was abolished, and the theological faculty in Prague was completely controlled by the communists, excluded from the union of Charles University and in 1953 moved to northern Bohemia, to the city of Litoměřice.

This was due to the strong entrenchment of religion in society and its influence on the population. In 1948, 73 % of the population of the Czech lands were members of the Catholic Church and around 20 % were members of other churches. Especially in rural areas, the majority of residents continue to attend religious services. But the ultimate aim of the regime was to entirely liquidate all religious communities.[4] After the removal of all Czech bishops from their sees, their imprisonment without trial and the liquidation of religious orders, the communist state practically declared a war on religion in connection with the violent liquidation of the private farming of peasants and their herding into cooperatives similar to Soviet kolkhozes.

The years of the strike against peasants and Catholics in the period 1951–1955 are often described by some historians as a civil war declared by the state against its own population.

This was connected to riots in eastern Bohemia and western Moravia, during which many peasants and Catholics lost their lives, and richer peasants were forcibly relocated to completely different parts of the state. Several parish priests were executed at that time on false charges. Since 1949, several hundred Catholic priests and active laymen have been sentenced to imprisonment for between 10 and 25 years in monster trials.

During the two to three years that followed the communist putsch of 1948, army chaplains were individually dismissed without new ones being appointed. There was a similar process with prison chaplains. The last chaplains accompanied the victims of the communist show-trials to their place of execution by hanging up

---

4 *Tretera/Horák*, Religion and Law in the Czech Republic, 2nd edn., Alphen aan den Rijn, 2017, p. 27–29. See this publication for details concerning all parts of this paper.

until the year 1950, but not later. Dr Milada Horáková, a mother, lawyer and member of parliament, was accompanied to her execution on 27 June 1950 by Protestant clergymen. Between 1950/51 and 1989 spiritual care in public institutions didn't exist.

Catholic priests and the clergy of other churches were imprisoned together in communist prisons and concentration camps. *The second school of ecumenism.*

V. Changes after 1989

The situation changed after the Velvet Revolution beginning on 17 November 1989. After that, the constitutional changes made the renewal of religious freedom possible.

But it was difficult to renew religious freedom in practice, especially in public life. And it was difficult to introduce spiritual care in public institutions. Why was this? A large part of the atheistically minded society rejected the emancipation of religion and believers. Due to atheism during the communist era, the number of members of religious communities had dropped by about half, especially in rural areas. Members of the old regime continued to work in the state administration, they were numerous and continued to support each other. They opposed the re-establishment of religious institutions and spiritual care in public institutions. Parliament dragged its heels over the restitution of religious communities' property that had been stolen by the communist state: it was only resolved after more than 20 years in 2012.

Religious communities in the Czech lands have common interests in the economic and socio-political spheres. On this basis, they work together to build spiritual care in public institutions. *Another school of ecumenism.* This time in a democratic state.

VI. Legal and contractual provision of spiritual care in public institutions and current data

Spiritual care in public institutions is ensured by Czech constitutional law, international treaties and national laws. An important role is played by agreements concluded between the Czech Bishops' Conference and the Ecumenical Council of Churches and the relevant state body. Currently, agreements have been concluded in the areas of prisons, the army, healthcare, fire rescue services and police.[5]

5 For details see *Horák* (note 1), p. 129–140 and *Horák* (note 3), p. 124–130.

Recently, ministry in the armed forces has been flourishing, with 36 full-time male military chaplains and one female military chaplain from eleven Christian churches. In addition, there is also a group of three active reserve chaplains. The chaplains are officers. Main chaplain is usually colonel. The amended agreement was signed in Prague on 18 December 2024.

Prison chaplains are employees of the Prison Service of the Czech Republic and belong to ten different churches. Currently, 43 prison chaplains from eleven churches work in 34 prisons and detention centres. In addition, several hundred volunteers associated with the Prison Ministry, which is a Christian super-denominational organisation, work in prisons. The condition is that they have a mandate from their churches. The organisation is also involved in the care of released prisoners.

Some progress has been made in the social sector in the spiritual care provided to homes for the elderly and other residential services.

In 2020, the Czech Bishops' Conference and the Ecumenical Council of Churches concluded an agreement on spiritual care in the Police. An agreement between the Czech Bishops' Conference, the Ecumenical Council of Churches and the Police of the Czech Republic was signed on 16 December 2024. The chaplaincy is performed by police officers employed by regional police headquarters. Each in double employment: as a police officer and as a cleric or preacher.